THE ESSENTIAL GRANDPARENT'S™ GUIDE TO DIVORCE

MAKING A DIFFERENCE IN THE FAMILY

DR. LILLIAN CARSON

Health Communications, Inc.
Deerfield Beach, Florida

www.hci-online.com

We would like to acknowledge the following publishers and individuals for permission to reprint the listed material.

"U.S. Map: Estimated Proportion of Americans Age 18 and Over Who Were Divorced as of March 1997" by Rodger Doyle. Copyright ©1999 by Rodger Doyle. Reprinted by permission of Rodger Doyle.

"An Epiphany enables you . . ." is from *The Essential Kabbalah* by Daniel C. Matt. Copyright ©1995 by Daniel C. Matt. Reprinted by permission of HarperCollins Publishers, Inc.

"Love at First Sight?" by Cokie and Steve Roberts. Reprinted by permission of Cokie and Steve Roberts.

"The Courage to Divorce" by Peggy O'Mara. Reprinted by permission of Peggy O'Mara.

"Hold fast to dreams . . ." is from *Collected Poems* by Langston Hughes. Copyright ©1994 by the Estate of Langston Hughes. Reprinted by permission of Alfred A. Knopf, Inc.

"Tables Summarizing the Laws in the Fifty States" Table 6, "Third-Party Visitation." Reprinted by permission from *Family Law Quarterly*, volume 31 #4, Winter 1997. Copyright ©1997 American Bar Association. All Rights Reserved. Reprinted by permission.

"The Contemporary Family—It's a Classic Plight" by Anne Norberg. Reprinted by permission of Anne Norberg.

"Break the Mirror" by Nanao Sakaki is from *Break the Mirror: The Poems of Nanao Sakaki*. Copyright ©Nanao Sakaki. Reprinted by permission of Blackberry Books.

"The extended family is in our lives again. . . ." is from *Funny Sauce* by Delia Ephron. Copyright ©1982, 1983, 1986 by Delia Ephron. Used by permission of Viking Penguin, a division of Penguin Putnam, Inc.

"Two Generations" by Martin Buxbaum is from *Once Upon a Dream* by Martin Buxbaum, originally published by World Publishing Co. Martin Buxbaum died in 1991.

Library of Congress Cataloging-in-Publication Data

Carson, Lillian, date.
   The essential grandparent's guide to divorce : making a difference in the family / Lillian Carson.
   p.   cm.
Includes bibliographical references and index.
ISBN 1-55874-689-7 (trade paper)
   1. Divorced people—Family relationships. 2. Children of divorced parents—Family relationships. 3. Grandparent and child.
4. Intergenerational relations. I. Title.
HQ814.C348   1999
306.89—dc21

99–23526
CIP

"Essential Grandparent" and the logo 🔲 are trademarks and service marks of Dr. Lillian Carson.

Publisher: Health Communications, Inc.
         3201 S.W. 15th Street
         Deerfield Beach, Florida 33442-8190

Logo design by Lily Guild. Author photo by Joyce Sipple. Butterfly drawing by David Serena.

To Susan, Steve and Carrie
who share my life's adventures . . .
and fill my heart.

Contents

Acknowledgments

Grandparents today are on a new frontier. Peter Vegso, president of Health Communications, Inc., not only recognizes this phenomenon, but is pioneering with me. By asking me to develop a series of *Essential Grandparent Guides,* he validates my belief in the *essential* nature of grandparents and the value of addressing their needs.

Pioneering takes belief and hard work and I enjoy both, not only from Peter, but from all the good folks at HCI. As we continue our work together, we have deepened our friendships. I rely on the HCI family: the editorial staff, Matthew Diener, Christine Belleris, Lisa Drucker and Allison Janse, all of whom exhibit patience under pressure and remain responsive to my requests; Kim Weiss, Randee Feldman and Ronni O'Brien who get the word out; Terry Burke, Lori Golden, Irena Xanthos and the many others whose work makes it possible for me to follow my bliss.

My appreciation to my agent, David Gershenson, who joins me on my mission; to Shelley Flanders whose research and assistance made a difference; and my many dear friends who stand by with encouragement as I disappear into a project.

The solidarity of my family is my greatest blessing; their patience, love and support cushion my life. And my dear patient husband, Sam, keeps me going with nourishment for both body and soul and some editing to boot!

Throughout life's challenges I have always considered myself extraordinarily lucky. This is further proof.

Introduction

*"I've decided divorce is the most violent word
in the dictionary, and now I must
live with it all my life."*

MOTHER OF DIVORCED CHILDREN
GRANDMOTHER OF THREE CHILDREN OF DIVORCE

These words, spoken by a grandmother with two divorced adult children, resonate with the power of experience and have challenged me, as a psychotherapist and writer on grandparenting and the family, to inquire into the impact of divorce on grandparents—as parents of divorcing adult children, as the grandparents of their kids' kids and as couples who themselves divorce. The statement above that provides the catalyst for this book leaves no doubt that divorce causes pain to the whole family.

I have interviewed countless grandparents about their experience in the aftermath of their children's divorce. Each situation is unique, but one thing is abundantly clear: Grandparenting in the face of divorce definitely does not come naturally.

With a current 50 percent divorce rate, few families escape the heartbreak of divorce. When it occurs, divorce stirs up complicated emotions and tosses family relationships into disarray. This book can serve as a compass for grandparents who are confronted with the conflicts and changes in the family resulting from divorce. It will guide them and other family members as they navigate a maze of tough issues and emotions they never imagined.

I wish to make it perfectly clear that this book does not sit in judgment. There are no value judgments as to whether one should or shouldn't divorce. I think we would all agree that divorce is lamentable, even when it is clearly in everyone's best interest. There is no smooth sailing in its wake. When kids marry we hope for the best, but the global acceleration of divorce rates indicates that it is an increasing probability in marriages. Divorce is changing our families and our society.

Courting Divorce

A growing number of couples in developed nations are ending their marriages.

COURTING DIVORCE

More and more couples in developed nations are ending their marriages. Divorce rates per 100 Marriages

Country	1970	1990
Canada	18.6	38.3
Czechoslovakia	21.8	32.0
Denmark	25.1	44.0
England and Wales	16.2	41.7
France	12.0	31.5
Greece	5.0	12.0
Hungary	25.0	31.0
Italy	5.0	8.0
Netherlands	11.0	28.1
Sweden	23.4	44.1
United States	42.3	54.8
(former) West Germany	12.2	29.2

Source: *Families in Focus*, by the Population Council

When faced with their child's divorce, grandparents run the gamut of emotions. From shock, anger, embarrassment, guilt, fear and sadness, they can find themselves so overwhelmed by this family crisis that solutions evade them. Guidance through step-by-step exercises and tips promotes the understanding and encouragement for grandparents to assume their rightful place at the head of the family, even when it's their own divorce.

As a resource for grandparents and others (brothers, sisters, aunts, uncles and friends), this book will help you to find the help you need to maintain your perspective. Grandparents need to keep their heads when all around them are losing theirs and blaming it on each other.

This book offers protection from the pitfalls that lead to the alienation of children and grandchildren, especially your daughters-in-law and sons-in-law, and you will learn how to effectively use your wisdom of gathered experience.

Most importantly, this book will strengthen your resolve to keep the family together and to stay connected to grandchildren, even when the family extends and blends with former members and newcomers, when it is necessary to fight for visiting rights, when grandparents take over as full-time caretakers for grand-children or when grandparents divorce.

The practical, everyday concerns—*What will you do? What will they do? Where will they live? How will they manage? Will we lose access to the kids? What about the kids?*—are what hurt the most. Precious lives of all ages are disrupted. Particularly for your children and grandchildren, you've wanted them to have every-thing good in their lives and now this . . . a serious blow.

In times of trouble, passivity breeds despair while activity breeds hope. And hope is offered in this reader-friendly, free-of-psychological-jargon, practical guide. You will find inspiration and useful information during a turbulent time.

We grandparents are on a new frontier. As a grandparent spokesperson I have the opportunity to meet grandparents around the country. We are enjoying the greatest longevity in human history and are the fastest-growing segment of the population. We are all pioneers and need the courage to blaze new paths.

For today's trailblazing grandparent, this is the first in my series of topic-specific *Essential Grandparent's Guides.*

1

First You Cry

"I'm all cried out. . . ."

MOTHER OF DIVORCING CHILDREN
GRANDMOTHER OF TWO CHILDREN OF DIVORCE

"Happily ever after . . ." Isn't that the dream of brides and grooms? Once upon a time a boy and a girl met, fell in love, married and lived happily ever after. Is this merely a fairy tale? Does it ever really happen? Certainly, divorce is not in our dreams. Marriages begin with such hope and with a beautiful pledge of unity. Couples vow that their union is for better or worse, for richer or poorer, in sickness and in health, 'til death do us part. All lofty ideals. But somehow, between that pledge and the circumstances of real life, something happens—something that converts dreams into a harsh reality that dashes these good intentions. Despite high hopes for the future expressed at the time of marriage there is a 50 percent divorce rate. One out of two marriages ends in divorce. With such shabby odds, marriage is not a good bet.

But weddings continue. We continue to believe in marriage. We continue to believe in love. Perhaps we're hopelessly optimistic; in the face of the risks, we keep betting that we can beat the odds.

1

ESTIMATED PROPORTION OF AMERICANS AGE 18 AND OVER WHO WERE DIVORCED AS OF MARCH 1997

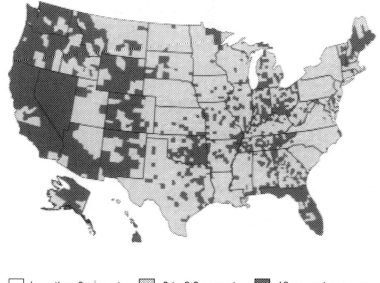

☐ Less than 8 percent   ▦ 8 to 9.9 percent   ■ 10 percent or more

Copyright ©1999 by Rodger Doyle

According to Rodger Doyle, in his article in Scientific American *(March 1999), the reasons for regional disparities are not definitely known, but they probably reflect several factors, including church membership and migration. This map shows higher divorce rates in urban areas.*

Recently, I attended a reception to celebrate a marriage. Held in the groom's parents' home, this happy occasion was filled with hope for the couple's future. The bride and groom had created an artful bookmark as a memento for each guest. The groom had rendered a butterfly for the bookmark as a symbol of their hopes, expressed in the accompanying poetry by Daniel C. Matt:

An Epiphany enables you to sense creation not as something completed,
 but as constantly becoming, evolving, ascending.

This transports you from a place where there is nothing new to a place where there is nothing old,
 where everything renews itself,
 where heaven and earth rejoice as at the moment of Creation.

Kelley and David
July 18, 1998

What a hopeful sentiment for evolving growth! The celebration was a communal expression of encouragement as each guest wished the new couple well with hugs and gifts and excited expressions of good wishes. In this day and age, getting married is an act of courage. As I observed the happy couple, I pondered their lives together. What would their challenges be? Where were the pitfalls or strengths that would determine to which group of statistics they would belong?

I noticed that the bride's parents were not in attendance although they live less than one hour away. I remembered that the groom had been married before to a seemingly lovely young woman who left him suddenly with little explanation. Both bride and groom are in doctoral programs at a nearby university—he in computer science, she in theology. Could this be a nourishing combination of science and soul or a future clash of worldviews? I do not know this couple well enough to hazard a guess. They are both likable. The groom's parents are my caring friends and I, like they, hope for the best. Who knows? Only time will tell.

Three Little Words

"We're getting divorced." That declaration changes everything in the family. The reality of your kid's divorce is a shock, even if you've known trouble was brewing. Marriages have their ups and downs. We keep hoping that it's only a temporary thing, a rough patch. Many parents have had the problems kept from them. Often their kids don't want to disappoint them, or they may be afraid they'll hear, "I told you so." And some just don't want their parents' input; they want to make the decision on their own.

Most parents are heartbroken. Their common reaction is to ask "Why? What went wrong?" Parents, grandparents, relatives or

"When I became a grand-parent, I never expected I'd be facing problems like these."

"Looking back, I know I did it all wrong when my son and daughter-in-law divorced. I let them all know how devastated I was, which burdened them and caused the very thing I was most afraid of. They shut me out."

GRANDMA MADELEINE

friends of a divorcing couple seek understanding in an attempt to gain mastery over a situation in which they have no control. "If I can grasp the reason this happened, I can make sense of it" is the hope. "If I make sense of it, I will somehow feel better or less threatened." We seek closure as we ponder the situation and ask questions. But beware. In attempting to understand what happened, placing blame becomes easy. We must bear in mind that as outsiders looking in, even if we are the parents, our judgments can be off-base. We are entitled to our opinions, but we must be very careful about expressing them.

In 1998, there were 1 million divorces in the United States. It is anticipated that this number will be equaled in 1999.

Grandpa Greg and Grandma Deb confided, "Dr. Carson, you are the only one who knows about our daughter's divorce outside of one close friend." These grandparents live in a small midwestern town; their daughter, son-in-law and two granddaughters live a four-hour drive away in a small farming town. "I know it's denial," confessed Grandpa Greg. "But it hurts so much and we keep hoping that they'll get back together, although there's almost no chance.

"We really refuse to believe it's actually happened. They called us on a Sunday evening and announced they had seen a lawyer and would be granted a divorce the following week. I didn't think you could get a divorce that fast. It left us feeling helpless and, worst of all, with a sense of hopelessness."

The grandparents continued, "There were some innuendoes about problems in the marriage but we were not suspicious. Two years ago our daughter got a job. She started receiving attention from the men at work. Naturally, she enjoyed that but it also highlighted the fact that her husband was impatient with her and called her stupid. They didn't know how to communicate."

Anguish to Anger

Some parents may complain, *"What more does she want?"* or *"He's a fool to leave such a lovely wife and kids"* or *"What are they doing to their kids?"* Some look to their faith for answers. "I believe they were falling away from God," said one set of grandparents. Yet no one really knows the problems but the couple themselves. Sometimes even the one being left is in the dark. "Why are we getting divorced?" I heard a husband ask his wife. This fellow really hadn't a clue about the causes underlying his impending divorce. The shock of it was devastating for him and an example of an obvious breakdown in communication. In this case, it is easy to see how this husband's parents could feel justified in blaming the wife, their former daughter-in-law, for the whole mess. But the fact that this poor fellow was in the dark may provide a major piece of the puzzle: lack of communication, perhaps lack of sensitivity, inability to connect to others. . . . Who knows?

Grandpa Howard was so devastated when his son and daughter-in-law divorced he literally couldn't talk about it. He left a note at our front door late at night explaining why he hadn't returned our calls.

So beware of jumping to conclusions. Even when you feel you know what happened and you know who is to blame, remember that you may be off base. Our questions may be unanswerable. Perhaps we even ask the wrong questions.

Don't Ask, Don't Tell

Some divorcing couples have strong, personal reasons for not wanting to tell the real reasons for the split, even to their parents. As a psychotherapist, I have heard many stories by a divorcing partner who wants to keep those details private. Often they want to protect their future by keeping damaging information from their children and others. Also, it may be an attempt to keep family relationships intact so that a spouse who has behaved badly is not ostracized—their ability to earn a living not compromised—or to keep the children from being tainted by their acts. Because these stories could cause scandal or shame, they may never be divulged. People outside the relationship might be less critical of some divorces if they fully understood the entire situation.

Here are the stories of four couples whose high hopes for their unions were dashed by a clash of values and shattered trust. They are reminders that we may not always see the whole picture.

The first is the story of Emily and Brian. When they were expecting their second child, Emily received a bombshell phone call from a young woman who told her that years ago, when the caller was a child, Brian had fondled her sexually on repeated occasions. She was coming forth now in an attempt to overcome her anger and resolve this trauma. Brian a pedophile? He didn't deny the allegations and admitted that he had not told Emily because he was afraid she wouldn't marry him. Emily was deeply shaken but determined to maintain a home life for their daughter and unborn son.

Try as she may, for over six years she could not overcome her shock and revulsion. Suspicion had replaced trust and eroded their relationship. Emily kept this story to herself, fearful that it would adversely affect Brian's employment. She worried that knowledge of these acts would be psychologically ruinous to the children and their relationship with their father. She also knew it would cause a breach in his cordial relationship with her family. For the children's sake, she wanted to maintain the best possible family situation. Finally, she filed for divorce. She and Brian have joint custody of the children, and he is a devoted father. To this day, no one else knows the truth behind their divorce.

In the second example, Marilyn was overjoyed to be marrying again. She had chosen William carefully after her first marriage to a flamboyant, high-living lawyer who became addicted to drugs and then left her. William, she felt, was steady: a stable family man and good provider. He ran an established business, owned a home and, since he had never married, was free of marital baggage. Besides, he was crazy about Marilyn, a beautiful and gentle young woman in her thirties, and her five-year-old daughter.

Both sets of parents were pleased, and William's parents helped solidify the new family with their enthusiastic embrace of their new granddaughter. So, what went wrong?

At the time of their marriage, William was facing major financial problems that he withheld from Marilyn. As they gradually surfaced, she began helping in the business. Unfortunately, the problems were serious and the business was in jeopardy. Marilyn's trust in William was shaken to its core. She struggled in disbelief with anger at his dishonesty. She had been betrayed. She worried that she was being materialistic but realized that it was his lack of openness and misrepresentation that had destroyed her faith in him.

She did everything she could to help him, working long hours in his office. But when she began to notice that she was drinking too much and that William's secretiveness continued, she realized that trust could not be reestablished, thus marking a sad ending to what had seemed a promising union.

Women initiate divorce more than half the time.

This next story is one of unheralded courage by a proud mother determined to protect her children and uphold family togetherness as much as possible so that her children would continue to have a relationship with their father. Resolved to extricate herself and them from an intolerable situation, hers is a story that others will never hear.

"I was appalled to discover that Stuart was planning a cover-up with his controller over what was actually an honest accounting error in his business," said Marie, Stuart's attractive wife and mother of his three young children. "I pleaded with him to just admit the truth, that he didn't know why there was a shortfall in his division. Once your credibility is compromised it is never fully regained." Stuart remained unconvinced and proceeded with his plan, and Marie was panicked by his willingness to put himself in jeopardy.

Stuart is what we psychotherapists call an *as-if personality,* a person who appears to function normally but is missing a core sense of self. They make choices based on expediency rather than relying on an inner moral compass. The resulting behavior is unpredictable and often socially deviant.

Marie did not want to undermine Stuart's future or his standing in the community. She wished to protect her children and herself from guilt by association and impending disgrace. "After all," she explained, "our futures are tied to his." Over time the abhorrent behavior patterns became more evident. They affected his parenting priorities, their relationship and her health. To protect Stuart and her children, she has never explained the real reasons to others and was widely criticized by those who could not understand why she would leave this marriage, especially with small children. Keeping her own counsel, she has never divulged the details. Stuart became more of a father after the divorce and is now a proud grandfather. This divorced family has remained separated but connected.

The last story may be aptly summed up by the old adage, *"Act in haste, repent in leisure."* Greg and Gloria's whirlwind romance culminated in a romantic wedding for the happy couple, but the revelations that followed were devastating. Greg was shocked to discover that his bride had made porno films and was plagued by thoughts of what else she hadn't disclosed about her past. The fact that she was pregnant with their child complicated the situation. Could he forgive her? He wasn't sure. They are together for now. He is concerned for his unborn child and vows, whatever happens, he will never divulge his wife's past. They are a couple on the brink.

The greatest challenge in these marriages is the loss of trust between the partners. Trust is the basis for a relationship. Without it, the foundation is unstable and relationships erode and wither. Secrets that accompany divorce are many: mental and physical abuse, sexual fetishes, mental illness, character disorders and social deviance. Living with any of these conditions is damaging and potentially dangerous to a spouse and family.

Be wary of judging others. You really never know what another's life is like. Don't demand to know the whys of a divorce.

Such knowledge is not your right. The fact is that most people who divorce view it as a last resort, especially when children are involved. Honor that with your compassion.

If we could step outside our own feelings, we might begin to understand differently and be led away from judgment and criticism toward lending support with an outstretched hand and a simple response such as, "I'm so sorry that you have had so much struggle that it has led to divorce." Such an empathetic expression will go a long way toward creating a connection to our divorcing children and paving the way for the future relationship.

"I keep my mantra in mind and repeat it often. 'I am not in charge.'"

GRANDMA LILLY

Content yourself with the ambiguity of not knowing. Perhaps it will gradually become evident. Perhaps not. As much as you might wish to, it is not your place to fix it. Parents need to learn the life-long lesson of relinquishing control.

"I'm sorry, Charles, but I've grown and you haven't."

©1999. Reprinted courtesy of Bunny Hoest and *Parade* magazine.

2

Redefining Marriage

"We settle down as man and wife to solve the riddle called 'married life.'"

COLE PORTER

A New Definition of Marriage?

Because divorce rates are increasing around the globe, some sociologists are suggesting that we begin to look at divorce beyond the individual and family and view this phenomenon as a cultural change.

In the new millennium, will the institution of marriage be defined differently? Perhaps, but in which direction is it headed? Will the pendulum swing backward, away from divorce?

A report from the U.S. Bureau of the Census shows that the average age for a first marriage has gone up from 20.8 years in 1970 to 25 years in 1997 for women and from 23.3 years to 26.8 years for men. Is this an attempt by Generation X to exercise caution?

Research by Larry L. Bumpass of the University of Wisconsin has determined that the divorce rate has stabilized in the past two decades. As of March 1997, the United States had more than 19 million divorced people, or 9.9 percent of those eighteen and over. Among whites, 9.8 percent are divorced, compared to 11.3 percent of blacks and 7.6 percent of Hispanics.

According to Mark Dunlap of the Relationship Institute of Santa Barbara, "Serial monogamy is wearing out. People are tired of changing partners. They realize how hard divorce is on children. They went from the ''til death do us part' before the 1960s to the stage where it was okay to divorce and even the *We all start out with great* thing to do in the '70s and '80s. Now," he says, *expectations.* "there's a trend back to the stronger sense of commitment. More couples are opting to work on their marriage rather than heading for divorce court." That sometimes means taking a serious look at their models for marriage.

Political reporters Cokie and Steve Roberts provide such a model with their answer to the question, "Do you believe in love at first sight?" They responded, "We believe in like at first sight, even lust at first sight. One glance can make your hormones go snap, crackle and pop. But love is a bit more complicated. We've been married for thirty-two years, and in love a lot longer than that. It's our experience that love takes time and tears, not just chemistry. Strolling on a starlit beach, holding hands and planning for the future is a loving experience. But so is sitting at the bedside of an ailing parent, holding hands and remembering the past. The key is staying connected and committed, day after day. That's real love."

Marriage reaches beyond the two partners. It encompasses a bond to a larger society as a public statement of intent to become a family. The family is the foundation of our civil society. And grandparents provide the cornerstone of that foundation. This is true in both a literal and metaphorical sense. The cornerstone is traditionally the first stone to be set, marking the beginning of the building. It is the repository for the history of the building, commemorating when it was built and those who contributed their efforts to its construction. And, standing at the corner of the foundation, the cornerstone provides for the convergence of the sides, joining and blending them together. And that's the grandparents' position. As the cornerstone, we are set first in time and hold the knowledge of the family history, the stories, the traditions and values that are a family's foundation. As the cornerstone of the family, grandparents serve the function of connecting their families, drawing and holding them together. Grandparents strengthen families.

"As the family goes, So goes the Nation."
POPE JOHN PAUL II, ST. LOUIS, 1999

Of course, many marriages are in serious trouble. Some divorces are, in fact, acts of courage. The following excerpt, written by Peggy O'Mara, editor of *Mothering* magazine, expresses the motivation, desperation and thoughtful resolve behind some divorces. It is a moving description of the struggle for growth in life and divorce.

> *I would like to refute the popular misconception that divorce is an act of cowardice, a running away, an easy way out. It is, in fact, a great act of courage when it has as its motivation the continued growth and health of the family. Divorce willingly and knowingly brings hardship upon the family. It is an open invitation to a hurricane. It is a purposefully chosen healing crisis.*
>
> *The self-inflicted natural disaster of divorce changes many lives irrevocably. It is painful, embarrassing, depressing, exhausting and often expensive. I do not believe that anyone would choose it who was not severely oppressed emotionally, psychologically, physically or spiritually.*
>
> *In measuring the varied impact of divorce, it is difficult to determine exactly how the many factors involved affect each of the family members. There are negative effects, such as the death of the nuclear family and the psychological sense of failure, parental separation and fear of physical separation, and positive effects such as relief from the violence or rage that may have*

> existed in the home prior to divorce, as well as the tension and
> disharmony.
>
> It is important to appreciate that families who are able to
> recover from the pain and disappointment of divorce can indeed
> be healthy and happy families again, and can even be healthier
> families. This does not mean that I encourage divorce or that I
> believe the positive qualities of divorce will drive hordes to the
> divorce courts. We are better than that! We do not give up easily.
>
> PEGGY O'MARA

Making a Marriage

Today's mind-boggling technology continues to remove us farther and farther away from the processes of life and complicate the
making and preservation of marriage. Urban
children, especially, are separated from the natural facts of life. For them, milk comes from the
market. A connection to the cows that produce
the milk products they eat and drink evades them. Much is lost by
this separation from the cause and effect of daily life.

*barn's burnt down . . . now i
can see the moon*

MASAHIDE

A minister friend recently lamented about our sanitized life
experiences. Recently on a trek in the Himalayas, she witnessed a
burial ritual where the family carried the deceased body to the
edge of a river that flows into the Ganges. After special preparation they burned the body and cast the remains to the waters,
returning it to nature. This hands-on experience confronts the
mourners with the absence of life in the physical shell as they are
giving it up to nature. It connects the living to the fact of death
and the cycle of life and challenges the wish for denial.

Contrasting this to the burial services she performs here in the
United States, the minister wondered out loud, "How did we get
so clean?" Mentioning that she usually asks cemetery officials for
dirt so that she can symbolically relate the return of the body to
the earth, she told me that sometimes she receives sand instead
because, it is explained, "It's cleaner." Adherents to the Jewish

faith have the tradition of lowering the body into the earth and shoveling earth to cover the coffin. Ancient Native American tradition returned the body to the earth directly, without a coffin. The early Plains Indians built a platform and left the body for nature's disposal.

Being removed from the life process affects our daily life and perceptions. It spawns disregard for the environment and leaves us unconnected to the life cycle. It has encouraged the quest for eternal youth at the expense of a reverence for aging and the value of older people. It also leads to some of today's mismatched marriages.

A wedding photographer told me of her interesting vantage point on marriage. She photographs about thirty weddings each year and interviews each couple. "About eight of those thirty marriages appear to be solid, a union of two people who have found their soul mates," she stated. "The rest seem to lack depth. Typical responses from them when I ask "Why are you getting married?" are *"Well, I'm getting older and I want to have children," "I've made it and it's time to settle down and have a family,"* or other vague answers that have to do with superficial aspects of the other person like *"He's such a fox," "I'm proud to have such a pretty fiancée."*

"Overall," the photographer continued, "I've been struck by the naive approach to relationship, the major issues that haven't been resolved, especially in mixed religious and cultural unions, the materialism, and apparent lack of depth in the relationships."

In their book, *The Good Marriage: How and Why Love Lasts,* Judith Wallerstein and Sandra Blakeslee enumerate the emotional tasks that couples need to complete in order to have a good marriage. After interviewing fifty couples who felt they had good marriages, the authors identified several psychological steps that couples must take to commit to a working marriage. The steps include *separating from the family of childhood, carving out autonomy,* and *creating an environment where anger and conflict could be safely vented.* All of the couples reporting good marriages had addressed these tasks.

It seems that many couples today have fallen in love with love without really delving into the tough issues. Perhaps it was always thus. Sad, unfulfilling and abusive relationships have existed forever. Perhaps as some have suggested, the 50 percent divorce rate represents a societal shift of raised expectations. But in this age of advertising we are often seduced to pursue a *lifestyle* (the right clothes, wines and car) instead of pursuing a *real life*. We are removed from the recognition of what really gives life meaning: real relationships and the ability to give and receive love. Life is not defined by major events or our possessions.

"All the unfulfilled desires for love, union and closeness find their satisfaction in the consumption of these products (love stories in the media: movies, TV, books, songs, etc.)."

ERICH FROMM

The beautiful wedding, the big diamond or other material things are no guarantee. Life is composed of a myriad of daily, routine events and experiences such as thoughtful kindnesses or irritations; the civility we extend to one another; the way we communicate our feelings—angers, frustrations, joys and love; how we listen, show care or turn away; and our willingness to accept those things we cannot change.

For the first time in history, human beings do not have to marry for money, property, social status, safety or the legitimacy of children. We're new at this relationship stuff. We're new at communicating honestly as men and women. The word *communication* was not even mentioned in marital literature until the 1950s.

A more positive view of the current divorce rate is that it is a result of social change rather than a cause. Families are trying to survive and evolve within a rapidly changing society. The movie *Pleasantville* highlights these social changes by depicting positive and negative aspects of the past. While showing sentimental love as pseudo-love, a love that is experienced only in fantasy and not in the here-and-now relationship to another person who is real, it offers a balanced view of the advantages that restraint and stability provided the kids growing up in the 1950s. But there's certainly no going back to *those good old days* and, obviously, we must be careful not to glamorize them. The movie effectively contrasted the lack of self-expression in the '50s to the increasing awareness of feelings and interpersonal communication of today by contrasting black-and-white images with those in burgeoning color to effectively demonstrate the growing intensity of aware-ness and self-expression over time.

One social scientist suggests that alienation in marriage begins with contempt, and that contempt arises when one partner becomes flooded with the other's negative emotions. Sometimes we can learn new ways to express negative emotions. Sometimes we are incompatible.

John Welwood, in his book *Journey of the Heart,* speaks elo-quently about the challenging path of true love. Many of us marry without realizing what marriage is or what it requires in terms of personal compatibility. Many of us marry for lust, for our church, for our parents, for our society, for our ideas of the pretty picture. Some go on to divorce because, ironically enough, marriage has given them the comfort to discover their true selves and, much to their dismay, disappointment or amazement, life may have something else entirely in mind for them.

"Life is so daily."
GREAT-GRANDMOTHER
ROCKING ON THE PORCH

Clearly the expectations of a person entering a marriage will help determine what kind of a marriage it will become. Perhaps it is our attitudes and expectations of marriage that lead us to dis-solution. A realistic view of family members will actually help you to enjoy them more and will encourage acceptance of inevitable imperfections.

Expectations shape our experiences, for better or for worse. I am reminded of the story I heard from a woman whose cultural tradition dictated an arranged marriage. Her parents chose the bridegroom, whom she had not met prior to the wedding. "As a new bride I had no expectations for romance," she explained. "I just prayed that my groom would have some redeeming qualities and would be bearable. I was so grateful for each positive attribute I found. It has worked out well." She continued, "The Western way of romance expects everything and then becomes more and more disillusioned with the relationship."

Although I am not advocating arranged marriages, this example of how expectations shape experience certainly speaks to the inherent disadvantage of romantic expectations. Clearly a person's expectations upon entering marriage will help to determine what kind of a marriage it will become.

In his book *The Seven Principles for Making Marriage Work*, psychologist John Gottman concludes that the quality of the spousal friendship is the most important factor in marital satisfaction. Anger, he says, is not the most destructive emotion in a marriage, since both happy and miserable couples fight. The real demons in marriage are criticism, contempt, defensiveness and stonewalling.

Embracing Change

Grandparents whose kids are divorcing are enveloped by many negative emotions: a sense of failure, fear for their children, sadness, loss. But what about the positive aspects of change: the relief from unhappiness, the joy of a new beginning, the courage to change and the energizing effect of expectations for a better life? We need to find ways to embrace the positive as well, to heal our wounds and bind up those of our children and grandchildren. We remain the role models for our families; that is the task that is before us.

"Why do people tell me I come from a broken home? What's broken about it? I have two parents who love me and two homes to live in."
TEN-YEAR-OLD CHILD OF DIVORCE

"I'm so relieved that my daughter finally had the courage to leave her husband. I'm worried sick about her safety and the children. They escaped his last tirade by going to the women's shelter in the middle of the night."

3

Grandparents and Grandchildren Have a Lot in Common

"Grandparents and grandchildren have a lot in common. They have a common enemy."

The conspiratorial relationship between grandparents and grandchildren occurs because neither are in charge. Our kids, their parents, have the ultimate power. Grandparents and grandchildren are not powerless, though. On the contrary, grandparents' opinions and actions can make a difference, and children's feelings certainly command consideration as well. What we say and do usually carries an extra wallop because, after all, we're still the parents to our grown kids. But, let's face it, it's our kids, our grandchildren's parents, who call the shots.

I heard a delightful story about a four-year-old grandson that illustrates the dawning realization of the chain of command. Taylor was having a sleep-over at Grandma's. When Grandma announced, "It's time to go to bed. You know, your mother said you should be in bed by eight o'clock," Taylor paused. He puzzled over this for a few moments and then asked,

"Am I entitled to make a phone call?
I'd like to call my grandmother."

Printed with acknowledgment from *Senior Times*.

"But aren't you *her* mother?" In other words, "Who's in charge here, anyway?"

It is confusing, these changing lines of command. After all, we're used to being in charge. The parents were our kids. But now, as grownups with kids of their own, they must parent our grandchildren and we grandparents must relinquish control.

Parents are often forced into the unanticipated roles of disciplinarian and police officer, not what most of us wish for when we plan a family. But children's actions demand that of us. So, despite our wish for harmony and friendship with our kids, they push us to reprimand *("You need a time out"),* to cajole *("Let your sister have a turn")* or deny privileges *("You may not go to the party. It won't be properly supervised").* This is a frustrating aspect of the parenting role. The necessity of becoming a disciplinarian forces parents into a role they really don't want.

The good news is that grandparents are more likely to get their wish for camaraderie with their grandchildren. That is their gift to us. The very fact that we are outside the daily grind of discipline and law enforcement permits us the freedom to just be with our grandkids, to hang out and to talk things over with more freedom and a different perspective than their parents.

Grandparents must be cautious and avoid playing an adversarial role with the parents. We must never forget that we're not in charge, even when it hurts. Raising kids today is a tough job, and our kids need our support and caring. Our kids may ask for our input, but they are adults now and free to make their own decisions and make their own mistakes.

Reprinted with permission from Ashleigh Brilliant. ©1998 Ashleigh Brilliant.

The common bond that grandparents already share with their grandchildren is reinforced in their common responses to divorce. Recognizing these similar reactions has given me an even greater appreciation for the unique position of grandparents at a time of family disequilibrium. Use this awareness of similarities to provide a greater understanding of your grandchild's experience. Utilize it to develop an increased ability to empathize with your grandchild.

Both grandparent and grandchild are bystanders in the event of divorce, each impacted by events beyond their control. They have similar responses and their questions contribute to the formation of even greater mutuality. Grandparents understand their grandchild's experience since it mirrors their own in many ways.

When faced with the reality of divorce, the child often feels somehow responsible for the breakup and asks, *"What did I do wrong?"* The grandparent asks, *"How have I failed? I must have been an inadequate parent."*

Then there is anger. The child is angry that one of her parents is leaving her and may take it out on her custodial parent. *"Why can't you work it out?"* responds the grandparent, with a tendency to blame the in-law rather than their own child. Anxiety about the future follows, as each asks: *"What will happen to me?" "How will my life change?" "Have I lost my absent parent?" "Will I lose access to my grandchildren?"* And then comes the sadness of the loss they both share . . . the loss of the family, of broken dreams.

What can grandparents do? Because divorce stirs up so many emotions, it's wise to be cautious and think before you act. Keep your own counsel and avoid overloading your children and grandchildren with your own reactions.

1. First become aware of your own feelings, especially the disappointment and anger, so they don't pop out at the wrong person, place or time.

2. You are the symbol of family stability, when everything else is caving in. Your strength is needed to shore up the

family and provide a safe haven, with reassurance that all is not lost.

3. Be discreet. Don't tell your grandchildren all you know about the problems or all you feel about their parents' divorce; rather, become a listening post.

4. Listen to your grandchildren without taking the side of either parent. Remember, for better or worse, your grandchildren need both parents.

5. Work to provide a positive, supportive atmosphere. This is one of the best ways to maintain access to your grandchildren.

6. Build in some fun for your grandchildren. They need a break from the tension. Help them to continue their normal lives.

7. Avoid overloading your children and grandchildren with your own reactions.

Enhancing your ability to put yourself in your grandchildren's shoes is a shortcut into their thoughts, worries, fears and needs. Here are the similar responses that grandparents and grandchildren share when faced with divorce:

Powerlessness. Neither you nor your grandchildren are in charge. It is not your decision. You are both victims of decisions not of your choosing. This leads to feelings of powerlessness.

Anger. Both experience anger toward the divorcing parents and others who may be involved. There is a tendency to blame them.

Guilt. Grandparents and grandchildren feel that the divorce is, somehow, their fault. They feel blame and guilt and, perhaps, a sense of failure. They wonder what they might have done to cause the divorce and what they could have done to prevent it.

Sadness and Loss. Both grandparents and grandchildren feel a sense of loss and abandonment. They are sad and depressed over the fact that the family is changed forever.

Anxiety. They become anxious about the future and fearful about what will happen to them. Each has many unanswered questions that create all kinds of worries.

Your perspective as a grandparent is a great asset. Use it for understanding and to find ways to connect to your grandchildren. You can be certain that it is quite natural for both of you to be experiencing these feelings.

The Emotional Stages of Divorce

Divorce is an emotional death. There is a grief and mourning process for divorce similar to the grief and mourning in the experience of death. Divorce is a loss, the death of an intact family. The hoped-for psychological outcome in a death is for the mourner to incorporate the deceased's positive attributes and, by doing so, preserve their connection. The hoped-for outcome in divorce is the reconstruction of the family into a new and functioning form.

"If only I'd been better. If I hadn't gotten into trouble, maybe they wouldn't be getting a divorce."

Brad, age seven

Three pronounced emotional stages follow the death of a loved one. Experiencing these stages is natural and healthy. Each stage leads us closer to reconciliation and the acceptance of change. In divorce the stages are similar.

Stage One: Shock and Denial

This stage is characterized by disbelief. Denial often comes in the guise of hope that the couple will change their minds. Devastation accompanies this stage.

Stage Two: Grief and Anger

Grief is the result of the acceptance of the reality. One tends to sink into a depression. The frustration that accompanies the sense of hopelessness also brings anger toward one or both members of the divorcing couple or others who might be involved. Despite the negativity of anger it restores a sense of power and can reduce depression.

Stage Three: Acceptance

To complete the mourning process takes approximately two years and, like digestion, it can't be hurried. Acceptance permits dealing with problems at hand, reconciling the judgments and negativity, and working at reconstituting the family to make it the best it can be.

"Roles of young and old need to change to permit each to contribute more fully to social and economic progress in the twenty-first century."
UNITED NATIONS GLOBAL MEETING OF GENERATIONS, 1999

"I do not believe anymore that all children are mightily harmed by divorce. I know that some are more resilient to change than others. My younger children, who had few if any preconceptions about divorce, had an easier time than my older ones, who were aware of the stigma of divorce and afraid that their parents' divorce would be as ugly as those they had heard about from their friends."

PEGGY O'MARA

Let the similarities between grandparents and grandchildren and the stages of mourning form a framework for understanding your own and your grandchildren's reactions around divorce. Use them to connect to your grandchildren, assured that you do indeed have special knowledge of their experience.

"We develop through experience. Therefore, hardships and misfortunes challenge us. It is in overcoming mistakes that we touch the song of life."
BEATRICE WOOD

The Grandparent's Role

Parents are often tangled up in their own world of heartbreak, anger, and the urge to win or punish—harboring fears, worries and practical details of change—and are not as available to meet their children's emotional needs. That's the task for grandparents; even if you're long distance you can reach out, listen and find ways to promote health and growth.

At the time of their parents' divorce, most children are under the age of six years. We understand today that divorce is not a transient experience, dealt with only at the time of the breakup. It continues to be the underlying cause of adjustments through-out childhood and beyond. At each develop-mental stage the relationship between a child and his parents is reworked. These relation-ships are more complex due to divorce. It is important to remember that divorce is a life-long experience.

Because children's basic trust in their parents and their world is compromised during divorce, make certain that they can depend on you.

When parents are divorcing, children's emotional needs are inevitably neglected. Nurturance for the children is diminished while the parents are getting their lives together, and trying to nurture themselves.

While parents are fighting for the children, who's watching them? This is a time when grandparents are able to make a tremendous difference by providing as much care and nurturance as possible. Grandparents can cushion this transition for their grandchildren.

This list of children's feelings will guide your understanding:

Children experience a loss of parenting. They feel there is no one to support them, no one to listen.

Children feel abandoned. They don't get the supervision they need. This is especially true of teenagers. It can drive them into antisocial behavior like drug and alcohol use, and sometimes early sex (especially for girls who are seeking attention). Brain scans have established that teenagers respond with the emotional, feeling side of their brains, not their thinking side. Honor the fact that teenage emotions are different from those of adults. They think differently, like the teen who told me, *"When I decide to do something and think of consequences, I think, 'Oh, whatever . . .'. But my mother thinks of all the things that could happen."*

Children are lonely. There is a cumulative impact that continues beyond the time of breakup. They worry about their parents and don't want to burden them with their problems.

Children feel frightened. If one parent can leave another, then both of them might leave the child. There are so many unanswered questions: *"Where will I live?" "Will I have a new school?" "What have I done to cause the breakup?"*

Don't forget that your adult children need your support as well. This is a time for grandparents to give in every way possible.

Others with Grandparent Roles

Many aunts and uncles and even close friends tell me that they feel like they are grandparents. They find themselves in similar predicaments, caring about their nieces, nephews or young freinds, yet not in charge. Like grandparents, they often feel the frustration of watching parenting they can't abide. Most of them tell me they try to zip their lips and keep their own counsel. They see their roles as expanding experiences for the children by widening their horizons with outings, stories, books or just plain hanging out together. It *is* very similar to grandparenting. These caring adults and mentors have a significant influence on children's lives.

Tool Kit for Long-Distance Grandparents

The two Cs, *continuity* and *creativity*, will help you to bridge the miles. By continually reaching out and exercising your creativity to do so, you can be an effective long-distance grandparent.

During stressful times, no matter how your input is sent, it will be important. Here are some tips:

- Maintain contact by phone, fax, mail or email. Writing a letter is a gift that can be read over and over again.

- This is a good time to become an on-line grandparent. You'll find that communicating by email is convenient, fast and economical. It is especially effective with older children. Try it, you'll like it.

- Create common interests and activities to participate in across the miles: a book you are both reading and discussing, a hobby you are enjoying together (i.e. stamp collecting), sharing jokes, exploring a topic or current events. You can help a grandchild with her homework and by researching a topic for a school project.

- Send things for no special reason to say "I'm thinking of you" and encourage communication (i.e. newspaper or magazine articles, cartoons, stickers, a Beanie Baby or money for an ice cream cone).

- Remember your adult children need your attention. Clip articles, send cookies, a honey-baked ham or a personal memento that will have meaning. It's another way to send encouragement. Remain available as a long-distance shoulder to cry on.

Changes Over Time

There is a serious gap between the legal system and the best interests of the child. The court determines visitation and financial support based on the child's age at the time of divorce and

does not allow for changes over time. Further-
more the child is not consulted and has no say
in these decisions. Particularly as children get
older they want to be with friends on week-
ends, go to dances and participate in sports.
Forcing them to go to visit a parent at the

"I spoke to my daughter almost every day during her separation. There was one dilemma after another. It's such a relief that things are more settled now and the divorce is final."

expense of their own social and skill development feels to them as
if they are being punished. And they are!

These children need advocates who, at the very least, can listen
to them and acknowledge their right to their own feelings in these
matters. The visitation arrangements for young children should
be flexible enough to bend and change as the child grows and
changes. When they are not, the child's normal life and needs are
disrupted.

Child support ends at age eighteen in all but five states. (In
Massachusetts, for example, it continues until age twenty-three if
the child is in school.) This leaves children cut off from support
at the time when they're ready for college and career education.
The courts have not addressed this situation, and few fathers are
willing to continue to help with college tuition, resulting in limited options and career choices for these children.

An issue I have never seen addressed is that of inheritance for
children of divorce. It is rarely provided in divorce settlements.
Inheritance is equated with love. If a child isn't remembered in a
parent's will it is tantamount to a withdrawal of love and acceptance, an ultimate rejection. Whether the sum is 5¢ or $5 mil-
lion, a child of any age should be protected from the deep
psychological hurt that results from being left out of a parent's
will.

As a grandparent, although you are most certainly not in charge
of the divorce arrangements, you can have some input by raising
these topics. At the time of divorce, your kids are pretty overwhelmed and most likely are not thinking of the far-ranging
implications for their children. Too often, the lawyers aren't either.

Issues such as medical expenses, life insurance, summer camps,

"A definition of civilization is the resolve to take care of those without power."
NOAH BEN SHEA

"What makes children so wonderful is they tell you what they know and stop."
MARK TWAIN

It is curious, but if one smiles, darkness fades.

schools, music lessons, church or synagogue membership, courses, tutors, recreational activities and equipment, special interests and hobbies should be on the list of things considered by parents, their mediators and legal consultants. Kids need these activities and experiences to help broaden and shape their lives and to develop their skills. These activities usually cost money.

Parents divorce because they feel it's best for them and ultimately for the family. But it is important to look beyond the immediate future and consider a child's long-range needs. As that six-year-old gets older her needs will change.

Things to Remember When the Going Gets Tough

Divorce is like a death and requires its own mourning process.

Consider counseling to help with painful emotions regarding this loss of family unity.

Grandparents should be sensitive to the children's issues and careful not to open wounds.

The effects of divorce continue through life and follow the developmental process.

Honor your heritage by passing it on to your grandchildren.

Support groups can help you cope with the loss of family unity.

Tough times don't last. Tough people do.

Hold fast to dreams
for if dreams die,
life is a broken-winged bird
that cannot fly.

Hold fast to dreams
for when dreams go,
life is a barren field
frozen with snow

LANGSTON HUGHES

Quotes from Children of Divorce

"When we were a family we'd do stuff together."

"They should get divorced because they were fighting. We don't know what's really going on."

"We're much happier now, now that they're divorced."

"I feel as if I'm missing out. I don't see my dad like I used to."

"I don't know why I have to go to my dad's and miss the school dance. It's not fair."

"Nobody asks me. It's all decided for me. Sometimes I'd just like to stay in one place."

"I have more fun with my dad now because he has a special time to see us."

"My grandpa is the one I can really talk to. He listens and won't tell."

"I received unconditional love from my grandparents. My own parents were so judgmental. Gram would fix me a chocolate soda at eight o'clock at night if I asked."

"I have fun at Grandma and Grandpa's. I don't have to worry there."

"Dad sings more now."

"When I visited my grandparents' farm in Tennessee every summer, things seemed normal. I was a part of a family. I played with my cousins and I loved the animals."

ADULT DAUGHTER OF DIVORCE AND ALCOHOLIC MOTHER

Grandchildren's Thoughts About Grandparents

We don't always know what to expect from our grandchildren, but here's how some third-graders answered the question, *What is a grandma and what is a grandpa?*

"A grandmother is lady who has no children of her own. She likes other people's boys and girls."

"A grandfather is a man grandmother. He goes for walks with the boys, and they talk about fishing and stuff like that."

"Grandmas and grandpas don't have to do anything but to be there. They're old so they shouldn't play hard or run. It is enough if they take us to the market where the wooden horse is, and have a lot of dimes ready. Or if they take us for walks, they should slow down past things like pretty leaves and caterpillars. They should never say 'hurry up.'"

"Usually grandmothers are fat, but not too fat to tie your shoes. They wear glasses and funny underwear. They can take their teeth and gums off."

"Grandmothers don't have to be smart. Only answer questions like 'Why isn't God married?' and 'How come dogs chase cats?'"

"Grandfathers don't talk baby talk like visitors do, because it is hard to understand. When they read to us they don't skip or mind if it is the same story over again."

*"Everybody should try to have a grandmother and grandfather, especially if you don't have television, because **grandmothers and grandfathers are the only grownups who have time for us kids!**"*

Tips for Communicating with Grandchildren

- Let your grandchild know that you want to help.
- Listen more than you talk.
- Don't push a child to talk. Don't pry.
- Without going into detail, express your own feelings honestly. "I feel very sad." This could give the child permission to express feelings.
- Give permission for the expression of feelings. It's okay to cry. It's okay to be mad. It's okay to have fun.
- Tell them, "I am here for you." (Even when you're long-distance you can be available by phone, fax, email, tape-recorded conversations, or cards and letters.)

- Encourage kids to speak about their feelings and what is on their minds. You can be their security blanket.
- Grownup problems cause divorce, children do not cause divorce.
- Talk about their many fears: *Why did Daddy leave me? Will Mommy leave me, too?*
- Ask them, "How's your schoolwork? Can I help? I'll take you to the library."
- Ask them, "Who do you like to play with? Would you like to invite your friend to go play? Would you like your friend to go with us?"
- Playing a game or reading a book to a child provides an opportunity for intimacy and communication.

Sweet As Honey

Grammy Betty described six-year-old granddaughter Ashley as "a smart girl with a big mouth and rather demanding." One day she decided to try something. Grammy asked Ashley, "Do you know about honey?" "No," Ashley answered a bit puzzled. "Well," Grammy continued, "honey is sweet and people like it. So, when you ask for things sweetly, like honey, people want to please you."

Grammy had no idea if she had made an impression, but, lo and behold, Ashley did try it out and began making requests sweetly. Happily, when she employed her new *sweet-as-honey* approach it was reinforced because it worked. Grammy was amazed and gratified.

4

Then You Get Ready: Your Personal Workbook

Why Make a Plan?

When there is a divorce in the family, the parents/grandparents are in the uncomfortable position of being controlled by events and by others. Although we're not in charge, we have an important role. Ours is often a supporting role, and we need to remain steady by keeping perspective and "being there."

It is easy to get caught up in our own daily tasks and neglect attending to the really important matters in our lives. Chores like getting the car fixed, going to the market, paying bills or getting to the dentist—not to mention work—occupy our days. That is why a plan is useful. It will help you to stop and think about what is most important. You can use the plan to organize your thoughts and stay on an even course. With a plan you can define your goals to ensure that you do what you most want to do. It can help to strengthen your resolve and intentions and shine a spotlight on possible pitfalls and trouble spots. A plan will help you become your best self by keeping your values and goals clear as you make decisions.

What Is Needed?

Step 1: Honest Self-Reflection

Step 1 requires taking time to sort out your thoughts and feelings. First, make an appointment with yourself. Our busy schedules make it easy to neglect our own needs.

"Become the change you want to see in the world."
MAHATMA GANDHI

Take this appointment as seriously as one you'd make with your friend, business associate or doctor in order to give this task priority over your competing activities.

Then, make a commitment to openness. This is a personal exercise. You need not be concerned about what others may think. Your answers are for your eyes only. Search your heart and mind for frank answers, for they will yield the most information and provide the greatest clarity.

When sorting through your thoughts, you can easily become overwhelmed by confusing feelings. A jumble of emotions needs clarification. Replacing confusion with clarity is a prerequisite for making good decisions and choosing a proper course of action to move forward.

Step 2: Recognizing Your Own Feelings: How Do I Feel?

"It does help to keep a journal: it forces me to be alive to challenge and to possibility."
MAY SARTON

Once you've made an appointment with yourself to undertake this important task, use the following checklist to help you identify your feelings. Begin by circling all the words that describe your experience.

shock

incredulous, traumatized, numb, futility, disbelief, dumbstruck

denial

expecting reversal of decision, resistance, unbelieving, nonaccepting

sadness

depression, despair, apathy, tired, exhaustion, melancholy, heartbroken, hopelessness, helpless, futility, downhearted, tearful, sleepless, lack of appetite

relief

"it's about time," alleviation of fears and worries, hopeful, understanding, resignation, satisfaction, thankful, grateful

worry

anticipation of future consequences, anxiety, uncertainty, fearfulness, instability

anger

murderous, vengeful, cynical, disgust, resentment, disapproval, disappointment, partiality, irritability, intolerance, impatience

guilt

embarrassment, personal failure, humiliation, confusion

burdened

obligation, financial demand, needing to rescue, must "make it better"

alienated

invisible, forgotten, pushed aside, defeated, conflicted, insignificant, lonely

detached

disconnected, impartial, "oh well" attitude

Additional thoughts and feelings: _____

_____

_____

_____

_____

Who Am I Blaming?

The Theory of Holes: When you're in one, stop digging.

Blame, anger and resentments are common emotions that block our path. They muddle our thinking, keep us going around in circles and, if unchecked, land us in a hole. People in holes have limited choices and lose their grasp of positive values, actions and goals. Are you stymied by being in a hole?

Answering questions such as *"How do I really feel?" "Am I blaming anyone for the problems?" "What can I do here?"* and *"What is my role?"* will help you get a handle on the complexities and is a step toward sorting out anxiety and depression.

Am I Blaming Anyone for the Problems?

Myself

My spouse

My son or son-in-law

My daughter or daughter-in-law

My grandkids

Others: _____

_____

_____

_____

_____

_____

Step 3: Acceptance

As we move through the stages of divorce—denial, anger, withdrawal, fear—even an eternal optimist can have a hard time seeing good in anything. It takes thought and adjustments to accept the new configuration of the family.

"Our whole country is surviving divorce."

The ability to heal and move toward our goals depends upon the acceptance of our feelings, no matter how uncomfortable or unacceptable they may seem. Remember, we're not responsible for our emotions, but we are responsible for our actions. Accepting our feelings with impartiality and without judgment (like a scientist views scientific data) paves the way for us to look at them objectively. This leads to understanding and growth.

"The old line of an eye for an eye leaves everybody blind."
MARTIN LUTHER KING JR.

Step outside yourself and take time to study your answers. Note the areas of conflict and contradiction. Mull it over. Meditate, pray. Talk about it with a trusted friend or counselor.

Remember, digesting feelings is a process that takes time. Just like digesting your food, you can eat fast but you can't hurry up the digestive process. It will take its own time. Don't expect to zip through these exercises. This is a process, so don't get discouraged.

There's not enough time to be nasty. We should be celebrating the smile of a child love of family . . .
There is not enough time."
BISHOP DESMOND TUTU

Opening Your Mind Through Forgiveness

What is getting in the way of my forgiveness? _____

_____

_____

What must I let go of in order to be free to act? _____

_____

_____

How can I forgive myself? (You must forgive yourself before you can forgive others.) _____

_____

_____

How can I forgive others? _____

_____

_____

Step 4: Setting Goals

"If it's going to be, It's up to me."

Before you can achieve your goals you must set them, and before you can set them wisely you need to decide what is most important to you, and in what order. Until you have a clear sense of what's important to you—your values—it will be difficult to make informed decisions and set goals. Examine the past as an aid to forging a better future.

"A journey of a thousand miles must begin with a single step."
LAO-TZU

What do I value most? Listen to your heart. _____

_____

_____

What is most important to me? _____

_____

_____

Do I see any solutions? _____

_____

_____

What do I want to do? _____

_____

_____

How can things get better? _____

_____

_____

What must I let go of in order to be free to act? _____

_____

_____

One of the advantages of getting older is the perspective we acquire. Pay attention to your wisdom.

Step 5: Action Plan

What can I do? _____
_____
_____

How can I implement my goals? _____
_____
_____

Writing for twenty minutes a day has been shown to have a positive effect on your outlook and health. As reported in the *American Journal of Medicine*, writing on a neutral topic is helpful but writing on a stressful topic has even greater significance in improving health by strengthening the immune system.

Goals for Grandparents

As you work through this plan strive for these attributes:

- impartiality
- honesty
- understanding
- love
- acceptance
- friendliness
- cooperation
- submission
- surrender
- peacekeeping

Communication Is a Basic Necessity for Your Plan

Say What You Mean, Mean What You Say

1. Create the climate

Pick the right time. Timing is key to reducing defensiveness and resentment. Pick a neutral time when there is an absence of negative feelings or anger. Spirits are darker at night.

2. Listening

Listen and make sure the other person knows you are listening.

Maintain eye contact.

Don't interrupt.

Ask questions to make certain you understand correctly and that you get the information you need.

Remain open; don't prejudge.

3. Think before you speak

Refrain from using sarcasm.

Don't accuse.

Allow for facesaving.

Don't burden your kids with your feelings.

Don't take sides or blame.

Empathize: "I'm so sorry you've suffered."

4. Consider options

Monitor your own defensiveness.

Avoid power struggles.

Don't try to be "right."

Ask for feedback.

Think creatively.

Remain open to new ideas.

Ask for suggestions on how you can be helpful.

5. State your intentions

I want to stay involved.

I want to support you in anyway I can.

I want to remain in my grandchildren's lives.

I'd like the grandchildren to know about their family and heritage.

I'd like them to keep in touch with cousins and others in the family.

I want to make a difference in my grandchildren's lives.

Please tell me how I can be helpful.

6. Make specific suggestions about what you'd like to do to help.

I believe it is in the grandchildren's best interest for me to remain in their lives.

I would like to help by . . . (be specific).

A bitter divorce can have unpredictable consequences for those who interfere. Ultimately, grandparents must be architects of their own future. You must come up with real answers for real problems. Proceed with caution.

Reconciling the Six Negative Emotions

Six negative emotions dominate us throughout our lifetime and certainly surface in members of a family going through divorce. In order to fulfill their essential role, grandparents must first reconcile their own emotions, including the negative ones.

1. Inferiority complex. We tend to compare ourselves to others. In doing so, we put ourselves down too much. Our compulsion to excellence can paralyze our actions by making us see elements and details that are not perfect. Interestingly, it is usually the high achievers who suffer from this the most. They are quick to critique their performance and recognize their imperfections.

2. Discouragement. Hand in hand with our high expectations is the letdown when our plans and serious efforts don't work out. Despite our good intentions we may not achieve our hoped-for outcome.

3. Worry or anxiety. Worry and anxiety become self-fulfilling prophesies that usurp our energy and cause us to go around in circles rather than progress on our path.

4. Guilt. Guilt is truly a great waste of time, and wasting time is one of the surest roads to negativity. It serves to erode our self-confidence as well as our focus for positive outcomes.

5. Resentment. Resentment and jealousy are very self-destructive. They cause us to hang on to negative thoughts, exacerbating our discontents. One of the psychological advantages we experience when holding on to our anger is a sense of power and justification, but it is a false sense that does not lead to conflict resolution.

6. Fear. Fear is insidious; it dominates the other five negative emotions. Fear easily spills over into anger and counterattack, causing a physiological reaction like that of a cornered animal who quickly turns aggressive and is ready to snarl and fight.

These negative emotions are inevitable when there is divorce in the family. But how can we protect ourselves? We need to learn ways to counteract these feelings and prevent them from controlling our thoughts and actions. As mentioned earlier, although we cannot be held responsible for our emotions, we are responsible for our responses and actions. By developing an emotional construct to immunize us from these inevitable feelings, we can teach ourselves to overcome and promote our own emotional health and that of our family.

Goals to Counteract Negativity

Begin by accepting your negative feelings and working toward the following basic goals that counteract negativity. Each goal represents an antidote, and each of them can be found in active grandparenting.

1. Add meaning and purpose to your life. The meaning added to our lives by performing our grandparenting tasks is unequaled.

2. Empowerment. By assuming our rightful position as an elder in the family we experience personal validation.

3. Connectedness. Strengthening intergenerational ties is healthy and keeps us young, in touch with the wonder of the world.

4. Hope. Children are our hope, and love is the greatest path to them. It is through them that our lives are extended beyond our time. The wisdom we pass on to them is our finest legacy.

"If I am all there is in my life, I should not have lived it."

MARIO CUOMO

IT'S NO JOKE, HUMOR HEALS

Almost thirty years ago writer Norman Cousins published *Anatomy of an Illness*, describing how he fought intense pain and beat a deadly disease by deliberately dosing himself with humorous books and reruns of *Candid Camera*. His story raised questions about the ability of humor to modify the effects of illness. Research by William F. Fry Jr., M.D., professor emeritus of clinical psychiatry at Stanford University, and Lee Berk and Stanley Tan of Loma Linda University, California, already suggest that "mirthful laughter" does much more than we think. Among other things, it can reduce stress by lowering levels of cortisol, a stress hormone that can weaken the immune system.

This is useful information for grandparents in their quest to reduce the stress that divorce visits on the family. Serve up helpings of humor to your family with books and stories, video- and audiotapes, or cartoons to bring some comic relief. And don't forget to hone your own sense of humor! How about telling some jokes to your grandkids?

Why did the boy throw the clock out the window? He wanted to see time fly.

5

Roll Up Your Sleeves and Fasten Your Seat Belts

"Activity breeds hope. Passivity breeds despair."

You've Got Work to Do

Grandparents have an important role to play in the lives of their children, as well as their grandchildren.

> *"My mother was married three times, so our family life was disrupted often as I was growing up. She didn't provide an example of how to remain a family. But my grandparents were always there modeling a good marriage and how a family could be together. I've been married for over thirty years, and I believe it is because my grandparents showed me how to do it. My five children have benefited from the loving home I learned to create from Grammy and PopPop. I was truly blessed to have them."*
>
> A RADIO-TALK SHOW CALLER IN GRAND FORKS, NORTH DAKOTA

The current information age overwhelms us with more information and stimulation than we can process. Today, one *New York Times* delivers more information to us than a person living in the Middle Ages received in a lifetime. Television brings the world into our living rooms and desensitizes us to war, violence and sex. Even with careful monitoring, our grandchildren see it all, with the undesirable effect of shortening their childhoods. As times change, so do cultural mores and so must parenting styles.

A child growing up today lives with a very different reality than that of her parents and one that is worlds away from the childhood of her grandparents. For grandparents to adapt to these changes demands flexibility.

The dual meaning of the Japanese symbol for change is threat and opportunity.

Your point of view determines your response and shapes your experience. If you resist change because it is threatening, your response will be protective and closed. When you define change as an opportunity, you are ready to openly embrace its possibilities.

As the pace of life accelerates, the generation gap widens. Grandparents often find these changes disappointing and painful. Our values may be called into question, and adaptation may require rethinking long-held beliefs and learning to accept family situations that do not fit our expectations. On the other hand, grandparents, by virtue of experience and position, have a broader, more philosophical perspective on life. We have an opportunity to be anchors for our family and bearers of our family's values and heritage, no matter what its size, shape or color.

The Four Most Important Tasks of Grandparenting

In a world where affection and allegiance are often conditional, simply giving and receiving love is a great gift. In fact, giving love is a grandparent's greatest offering. I have identified the four most important tasks of grandparenting. They are important no matter the grandchild's age and they define our grandparent roles.

1. **Unconditional love.** We offer unconditional love, accepting the child "as is." Our belief in them fosters their belief in themselves.

2. **Modeling a good life.** We foretell the future for our children and grandchildren. When we live our lives with vitality and enthusiasm, we tell them that life is worthwhile, that the future is good.

3. **Providing continuity.** Grandparents provide a bridge between the past and the future. We inform grandchildren that they belong to something greater than themselves. They belong to a family with a history.

4. **Providing stability and security.** *"A family is a place where, when you go there, they have to let you in."* Grandparents provide security and a safety net for their children and grandchildren—and a helping hand when they fall, to enable positive risk-taking.

In these ways grandparents influence the future. We give our grandchildren roots into the past and wings to explore the world. We need to seek new ways to offer these gifts when there is divorce. The situation may be changed, but the needs for all of our offerings remain the same.

When you aim for perfection, you discover it is a moving target.

Patch, Patch, Patch

This is how one grandmother described her role: "It's patch, patch, patch." I agree that's often the case. When family life is disrupted, grandparents end up with the job of smoothing things over, attempting to take up the slack or providing some moments of diversion. Patch, patch, patch sums up the position of many grandparents.

"They seem to go from one crisis to another and I keep trying to help make things better. It's discouraging, but what can I do?"

Another grandma described the differences between her daughter and herself. "I don't agree with the way she indulges her daughter. Those parental indulgences are contrary to my own sense of what's enough. The emphasis always seems to be on, 'Where is Cindy going to go next?' She's fifteen, and I think she needs some time to just be. Instead she was taken to London and Rome for two weeks at the beginning of the summer and then to Canada for summer camp. Each parent wants to be *the good parent,* which results in their outdoing one another with plans for their daughter. Cindy's stepmother is from

Keep life in perspective.

New York so they often pick up and all go there from their home on the West Coast. It may be very glamorous and exciting but I don't think this is preparation for real life."

This is, of course, an affluent family, but I believe Grandma has an important point of view. Cindy may, indeed, be a "poor little rich girl" as her parents lavish her with all that money can buy. To help them develop inner resources, children need some time to relax, time to think and time to just be.

When Grandma is with Cindy, she tries to provide such times. They take walks and cook together. It's Grandma's way of offering some relaxed, unstructured time. Since she and her daughter don't see eye to eye on how to raise Cindy, Grandma's best recourse is to provide the experiences she feels Cindy is missing. The results are much more positive than alienating her daughter with her disapproval.

The *Hurried Child* was first described by David Elkind in his book of the same name. Too many kids are overscheduled and hurried through life. Few parents ask *"What is the point of all this activity?"* One overscheduled ten-year-old boy's answer to my query, "Would you like to have more free time?" was "Oh, yes." Then, upon reflection, he added, "but I'm not sure I'd know what to do." This child is being robbed of the opportunity to find his own interests to fuel his choices. He is propelled by the schedule of activities that is imposed upon him. It precludes the time needed for self-discovery. A hurried grandchild needs a

"Mommy, why are we always in a hurry?"

THIS QUESTION FROM A FIVE-YEAR-OLD SHOCKED HER MOTHER BECAUSE IT WAS SO TRUE. THE MOTHER HAD NO ANSWER.

grandparent to provide unhurried time for exploration and self-discovery.

On the other hand, if the child does not have the advantage of outside stimulation, this becomes the need, and a grandparent can offer opportunities to make up the deficit. Grandparents can fill in the gaps. This doesn't have to be costly. For example, cooking or gardening or taking a walk with a grandparent provides the best of times. Reading to a child of any age nourishes your relationship while stimulating and educating the child. When deciding how you can make a difference in your grandchild's life, don't overlook the simple, everyday pleasures that nurture. [For guidance on reading to children see information for Dr. Lillian Carson's Essential Granparent's Reading Circle . . . for Grandparents & Others at the back of the book.]

Grandma Sue stated, "My daughter is the 'queen of drab,' and I'm into color. We're so different. I don't see her often but I try to give her and the other children experiences that might open them up to new and exciting ideas. Because they're long distance, I'm limited but I send magazine subscriptions like *National Geographic* and some political magazines. They give us something to talk about and get them interested in new ideas."

Grandma Jan told me how three generations—she, her daughter, and fourteen-year-old granddaughter—all went together to see the movie *Stepmom*. Afterwards, when we were talking about the film, Jan reported that her granddaughter said, "You know, I never thought about my relationship with my stepmom from her point of view, what it was like for her to suddenly have me in her life." Grandma was amazed at this revelation and realized that this was an important area for future discussion. It was evidently a little bit too loaded an issue for the mom to deal with.

These stories are examples of how divorce is not only about the breakup and getting on with your life. The effects of the dissolution of the family are far reaching and long lasting. Issues continue to confront the family, and are never ending.

Where's Daddy?

A current debate about the importance of fathers in their children's lives seems just plain silly at best and undermining and harmful at worst. Anyone who has worked with children, as I have, or had a supportive and loving father knows how ludicrous it is to question the need for a father. Children who have absentee fathers seldom forget that he is out there somewhere, that he has abandoned them and that, as one girl said, "He discarded me like garbage."

Today's fathers are usually more involved in parenting. Fathers and babies have more to do with each other than ever before. Compared to the previous generation, the proximity of fathers to their children is up by one third, and the time spent together is up by one-half. It has become more common for fathers to be caregivers.

The loss of a father's involvement is definitely detrimental to children. It causes emotional pain and loss of self-esteem. Grandparents, whether you're on the bride's side or the groom's side, you will be doing your grandchildren a service by facilitating their father's involvement, for they are critical in a child's development. Fathers are role models for their sons. Their support for their daughters is highly correlated with their daughters' achievements, and their support of the mother encourages her performance.

We know there are fathers so detrimental to their children's emotional and physical health that they must be banished from the child's life. When a father is threatening, abusive, unpredictable, involved in antisocial behavior or addicted to substances, he poses a danger to the children. In such cases it may be preferable to bar him from the child's life. Constantly reintroducing a toxic parent into a child's life keeps the child emotionally unbalanced and prevents healing. Seeing an abusive father is like opening a wound again and again. In their book,

"We try. We fail.
We try again. We fail.
We readjust our game plan."

The Best Interests of the Child, psychoanalysts Anna Freud and Albert J. Solnit and Yale Law professor Joseph Goldstein point to the need for the courts to recognize the wisdom of barring toxic parents (fathers or mothers) from their children. Children deserve to be protected.

How does the divorcing process contribute to the father's diminished capacity to parent? Fathers often feel displaced and awkward. Their fathering role must be redefined. They need encouragement to remain involved in their families, especially around the time of developmental touchpoints such as pregnancy, childbirth, illness, entrance into childcare, entrance into school, separation and divorce, adolescence and job loss. These are not neutral events. Every time a child experiences one of these landmarks the father should be there.

Unfortunately, subtle discouragements lead to a pervasive shame by fathers. They do not receive social support for their involvement, especially with small children. For example, one father reported that when carrying his new baby at the mall many women approached him to smile, see the baby and ask questions, while not one man came up to him or even acknowledged the baby.

A pivotal determinant affecting father involvement is employment. Ongoing employment is necessary for fathers to remain involved with their kids. Studies during the Great Depression of the 1930s (when unemployment was common) show how undermining this condition is to the family. Unemployed men suffered from a lack of self-esteem and were diagnosed with depression. Their relationships within the family, especially with their wives, deteriorated. As unemployment continued, disharmony increased, and, in many cases, led to divorce.

> *"Divorce is when Dad leaves, he never comes back and the family is dead."*
> SAM, AGE THREE

How can we create more "father-friendly" situations? Fathers need to support other fathers. They don't do that very well. Support groups for men can follow the model of the many support groups for mothers.

One of the big issues for dads is child support. And one of the major issues for moms and kids is deadbeat dads, fathers who don't contribute support to their kids. Because this has become a serious social issue, many states are legislating harsh penalties against these delinquent dads. Their lack of support creates emotional as well as financial stress for the family, often plunging them into poverty.

An area of awkwardness for fathers is play. Many fathers are uncertain how to play with children. It is easy to understand that a father who does not live in the children's home and has been less involved may not know much about the caretaking role and may be at a loss for what to do with kids for the whole weekend. Consider the following ways that grandparents can help him learn:

"Dad doesn't come to school anymore and he breaks promises."

- Offer encouragement.

- Offer to participate jointly.

- Give him tips for foods to have on hand.

- Supply him with toys and games and art supplies.

- Encourage him to read to children and suggest appropriate books.

- Give him ideas as to what to do with kids.

"My kids used to just sit and watch TV all weekend at their dad's. It was depressing."

- Encourage outdoor activities. Children need exercise for emotional and physical health.

- Give him a break during the weekend by babysitting for an hour or so. A weekend can be a very long time.

"As I watched my wife play on the floor with our grandbaby, I felt envious. I don't know how to play with a baby."
Pop-Pop Eddie

- Invite him to visit with and without the kids.

- Maintain your interest and support. Most single fathers are lonely and feel displaced.

- Let him know how important he is to the kids.

What Do the Kids Know and When Do They Know It?

In a study of children who were 2.5 to 6.8 years old at the time of divorce, Dr. Kyle Pruitt of the Yale Child Study Center found that the children had many questions they were unable to ask. When asked to draw the family, they usually placed themselves closer to the residential parent. Often the parents were shown with missing limbs, and one child placed his absent father on the back side of the picture. Children often spoke about traveling back and forth between Mom's and Dad's. Their play themes also highlighted this back-and-forth that changes their lives by taking them away from familiar neighborhoods, friends, toys and routines, and requiring adjustments to different parental expectations. One child created a visiting machine in his play. As Dr. Pruitt observed the children's play he noted other themes, such as children acting out telephone calls to the other parent, worries about keeping things safe, or as five-year-old Jason said *"keeping things even-headed."*

Children know what's going on.

Children's Definitions of Divorce

These quotes, from kids asked to describe divorce, reveal their point of view:

"I came from the time that they liked each other. It's over now."

"Mommy cries a lot."

"You take turns between Mom and Dad."

"You pay your lawyers a lot of money to wreck your family."

"Judges are paid to decide things when no one else can."

"Lawyers take a lot of money from people."

"Once they got lawyers they stopped being friends, just like that."

"I don't talk to them about my feelings much because they have so many problems of their own."

"We had to move. I miss my friends from my old school and my house."

"Judges shouldn't scare people about not seeing each other anymore. It's too scary."

"Judges should listen to kids. They aren't as smart as grown-ups but they know the truth."

It is clear that children understand what's going on. They are alert to the conversations around them. After all, their lives depend on it. Their statements reflect the dominant themes for children of divorce: loss, loneliness, sadness, fear, anxiety and disruption. The overall reduction in the parents' ability to take care of them and spend time with them is paramount. There is a direct correlation between the amount of conflict in the family and the depth and intensity of these emotions experienced by the child.

"Tough times never last.
Tough people do."
    Mike Utley, athlete with
       spinal cord injury

6

The In-Laws Don't Have to Become Outlaws

Discussions today are characterized by adversarial positions that polarize two points of view. Television is filled with people arguing their own ideas and not taking time to think or listen and consider the other's side. Such poor models for conversation and civility are guaranteed to keep us apart. We must be careful not to bring this popular mode of debate into our own lives for it does not lead to thoughtful problem solving or to finding solutions. It closes minds and separates people.

How do we come together? How do we maintain family togetherness despite differences and wounds? First, we must decide that we *want* to overcome the obstacles. We must be steadfast in our determination to hold the family together no matter its shape. When there are children, there is almost no such thing as total divorce. The children make it necessary and desirable for the divorcing couple and their families to have lifelong relationships.

The stories that follow are inspirational. They are the stories of grandparents determined to keep close relationships with their grandchildren and continue to influence their lives.

Grandma Sarah was determined to remain a presence in her two-year-old granddaughter's life after her son and daughter-in-law divorced. It became especially challenging when granddaughter Laura's mother remarried and moved to a remote area of Northern California, a long way from New York City.

Sarah made her intentions known to her daughter-in-law at the outset. She wanted to remain a positive force in Laura's new family. For a working woman, supporting herself, this took planning.

Her yearly visits to California were inconvenient and expensive but she persisted. She also remained a continual presence in Laura's life by sending her some important, useful gifts that would send the message that Grandma was thinking of her. She chose items that would be used often, like a computer and a boom box (a tape player/radio). Keep in mind that, for a woman on a limited budget, these gifts had to be carefully budgeted.

The plan has worked. Now in her thirties and married, Laura and Grandma Sarah enjoy a warm relationship. The pleasure of this connection also extends to her former daughter-in-law and her new husband. And Grandma has the satisfaction of knowing that she has strengthened the bonds between Laura and her father's side of the family.

Another story of steadfast support was told to me by Carrie who sells her homemade preserves at our local Farmer's Market. When I asked about her family, she told me that she had her former daughter-in-law and three grandchildren living with her. "My daughter-in-law is a twenty-six-year-old adolescent," Carrie said with her characteristic good nature, "so my son and I decided that it would be best for the children if they moved in with me." This is a twist on the grandparents raising grandchildren stories. Here was a grandmother who was raising her former daughter-in-law as well!

The story really begins in daughter-in-law Peg's childhood. Her parents divorced after her little brother tragically drowned in the bathtub. Peg's mother left her in the care of her maternal grandmother and faded from her daughter's life, so at fourteen she went to live with her father and stepmother in a household of hollering, abuse and alcoholism. Carrie described Peg as a person who seemed to have that extra something, "the spunk that helps to pull them out of the muck and mire." Peg saw education as her answer and was attending the community college in her Midwestern hometown when she met Dan, Carrie's eldest son. He admired her determination to have a better life, and they married.

After the marriage, Peg seemed compelled to recreate the violent household of her youth. She admitted to egging Dan on to lose his temper. Finally, as the situation in the household deteriorated, she yelled, "You get out of here," and he did. At this point they had two daughters, ages three years and thirteen months, and one on the way. Every time Dan went to visit, she would explode and throw things, making it impossible for him to move back.

Carrie described her relationship with Peg by stating "from the outset I accepted her. She had no real mother. We both knew I wasn't her mother but I was a shoulder to cry on." When Carrie went to visit after the divorce she found that Peg was not very functional. "I realized she wasn't finding a place to live and was having drinking bouts. I also worried about Dan's loss of weight. I suggested to my son that Peg and the children could come to live with me in California. It meant that he wouldn't see the children, but because of his concern for their health and safety, he agreed that I should invite her.

"When I invited her to come, I gave her three conditions I expected her to meet: get a job, pay something toward the children's upkeep and go for therapy. I thought it was important for her to take some responsibility. The therapy part never worked out. Peg arrived with a chip on her shoulder. Instead of working as partners, I was an antagonist.

"She stayed with me for a year-and-a-half and filled my house with negative energy. I ended up with the full care of the children, doing all the cooking, dishes and cleaning. It was emotionally and physically sapping me. She became abusive and physically lashed out at me, accusing me of trying to take the children away from her. As she became more and more unpredictable, it became clear that she had a drinking problem. I even ended up reporting her for child abuse after I overheard her hitting the four-year-old, leaving a hand-shaped welt on the little girl's face.

"Each morning I would brace myself to go forth from my bedroom by reminding myself, *I'm doing this for the children.* Peg is now attending the local university and has moved to student housing with the kids. She remains angry, alcoholic, abusive and in total denial. She is also very skillful at eliciting sympathy from others. Meanwhile, Dan has filed with the courts for custody of the three children. The court-appointed evaluator seemed to grasp the situation accurately, and we are 'cautiously optimistic' that he will get the children. If he does gain custody, the children will move back to the Midwest with him."

Grandmother Carrie is planning to help with that transition by returning with them. She will aid them in getting established, finding schools and day care, cooking and settling them into a routine. "My daughter is willing to keep my business going and work the market. We are a family working at this," she stated with pride.

"You must worry," I said sympathetically. She answered quickly. "No, I don't worry. I can't do any more than I've done. I can't worry about things I can't change. I've gone to a therapist and to Al-Anon for support. I've grown and learned some things about myself.

"You're very strong, Carrie," I responded in admiration. "My parents loved me. They gave me strength. And I had grandparents who believed in me."

"If you think you have everything under control, you're not going fast enough."
BARRY BERELOWITZ

Grandma Carrie's story is an example of a family's strength and resolve to help each other and keep the welfare of the children their priority. The next story is yet another example of heartwarming family solidarity.

"My son is moving back home today," a grandmother volunteered during my grandparenting class. "Right now, he and my daughter-in-law are telling their daughters (ages nine and twelve) that he is moving out." When we met again a few months later, her son was still living at her home.

"Before he moved out, we were at their home. My daughter-in-law was clearly distraught and crying as we did the dishes. She confided that they were having problems and that Jonathan wouldn't see a counselor. I took a risk and suggested, 'Maybe you need to see a counselor.' She didn't take offense and actually began to see one. When Jonathan moved out and asked to move back home, we were devastated. We knew they weren't happy but, after fourteen years of marriage, were hoping that with counseling they would work it out.

"When Jonathan arrived he was crying a lot and very depressed. The nice part is that we, my husband and myself, reestablished our relationship with our son. The three of us cried together, held each other and bonded again. Those first few weeks were difficult and exhausting with a lot of talking and crying.

"I hadn't spoken to my daughter-in-law, Lee. Jonathan reported that she felt terrible that we weren't talking so I called her. She was very pleasant but obviously guarded. It was a bit of a strain. Over time she told me she was learning that her relationships were always at a superficial level due to her difficulty getting close to others."

According to Grandma, "The grandchildren seem to be doing well. They haven't had to make any changes other than to get used to their dad not being there. They see him often. There was a lot of unhappiness in the marriage and the children see their parents growing hopeful that they'll get back together. The older one is pretty closed about it but the younger one asked me if I were mad at her. Maybe she is mad at me?

"I have questioned what I could have done differently that might have helped. Jonathan was unhappy for a long time. Should I have been more confrontational, more honest about what I saw? I didn't want to meddle.

"When Jonathan moved in with us I told him up front, I don't cook much anymore. You're welcome to have meals with us when we're home but you're on your own. And when the grandchildren come to be with him, I let him take responsibility for them and try to give them plenty of time to be by themselves.

"I feel a need to be there emotionally for the grandkids. Our communication is good and we spend quality time. They spend time working with their grandpa in his studio and we go golfing. I'm alert to their moods, and when they seem down I try to get them to talk about it. The other grandparents act like nothing has happened. They don't talk about it. We've never really had much in common.

"If this separation continues, we'll expect Jonathan to find his own place. As nice as it is to have him with us, I don't think it's healthy for him to stay indefinitely."

These stories really expose the emotional pain that grandparents experience during divorce and their tentative relationships with the in-laws. They also serve as models for the careful thought and diplomacy necessary to keep communication open and judgments and frustrations to oneself. One grandmother told me of the mutually reciprocal arrangement she enjoys with a friend. They have agreed to call each other to unload their frustrations about their kids so they can avoid saying or doing something they might regret later. Lets face it, being an in-law can be precarious.

It was easy to understand why the Hills truly adored their daughter-in-law Annie. She was lovely. Talented, kind and easygoing, she was also a devoted mother to her three children. When she and their son, Kent, announced their intention to divorce, the Hills were shattered and literally unable to talk about it. It seemed to hit Grandpa Howard the hardest.

What has been interesting to observe over the more than fifteen years since this breakup is the way Annie has truly remained a member of the Hill family. She is included in family gatherings and continues to be a devoted daughter-in-law. In fact, now that the Hills both have medical problems, Annie is the family member on call in case of an emergency. Neither Annie nor Kent has remarried, so new mates are not an issue, although Kent has had a girlfriend for many years who is also included. They have all put their interest in the children/grandchildren and their truly bonded relationships ahead of personal hurt. This inclusion is a model for a family remaining together despite the difficult circumstance of divorce.

Tips for Maintaining Your Relationship with Your In-Law Kids

- Reach out to your in-law child and state your intentions.
- Let him/her know that you want to remain involved with the grandchildren.
- State your desire to continue to have family celebrations.
- Indicate that you'd like to help out (give specific suggestions).
- Offer to volunteer in your grandchild's class.
- Express your sympathy for the situation.
- Don't place criticism and blame.
- Avoid getting in the middle.
- Don't burden them with your own feelings.
- Display your good will.

Forgiveness: An Act of Courage or Self-Denial?

"To err is human, to forgive divine."
ALEXANDER POPE

This oft-quoted saying recognizes the difficulty of forgiveness, for it must come from a deep place within ourselves, a place that accepts the imperfections in human nature while choosing to rise above them. It also comes from a determination to forge ahead toward higher goals by encouraging growth and a willingness to learn from life's lessons.

Why, then, is it so difficult to forgive?

"Without forgiveness there is no future."
BISHOP DESMOND TUTU

Because, somehow, at the base of forgiveness are the seeds of self-denial. If we forgive, if we let go of our anger and indignation, we experience a sense of betrayal to ourselves. Holding on to anger becomes a trap that hinders us from reaching our goals.

> *"I always had a pleasant relationship with my son-in-law, and now that he and my daughter are divorced we keep in touch. He came to visit me with his new wife and I look forward to meeting his new baby. I sent them a baby gift; after all the baby is my granddaughter Ashley's half-sister, and I don't want Ashley to feel that her two families are entirely separate."*

The Other Grandparents

The in-law grandparents also require thought. Even if you are not very close it helps to give them the courtesy of a call or note to acknowledge the divorce and the change in the family. It is easier for the grandchildren when the two sides remains friendly.

On the other hand, if you have a relationship with the other grandparents it behooves you to reach out to them. It may be awkward but, unfortunately, divorce creates many awkward situations. Like the predicament of grandparents Sid and Barbara. They enjoyed a special relationship with their daughter-in-law's parents Hannah and Jim. The four of them enjoyed each others company, going out to dinner, playing cards, and traveling together. It was a united family. The divorce of their kids was a shock. They were all heartbroken. It also precipitated a personal dilemma about the cemetery plots they had purchased together. They felt a joint gravesite would be easier for their children when, someday, they visited the cemetery, and also represented a symbol of unity between families. Now Sid and Barbara felt estranged from this notion and after much deliberation

"Moral recovery cannot be done in an unloving way."
Reverend J. Philip Wogaman

decided to sell their plots and purchase new ones in another cemetery. It was a sad loss for the family. Another rupture resulting from divorce.

The four attempted to hold on to their former camaraderie but their relationships were obviously strained by their kids' divorce. They still enjoyed comparing notes about the grandchildren but couldn't help but experience discomfort as the divorce progressed and controversy between their children surfaced. In divorce, the grandparents are often the forgotten casualties.

7

Fight For Your Rights: Grandparents Are Essential

When There Are Problems in the Family

When there are problems in the family preventative measures are your first course of action. Keep your objectives in mind. Divorce is highly charged with emotions, so don't hesitate to make amends with an apology, when it's in order, even if it hurts or doesn't seem quite fair. Keep your eyes on the prize: the welfare of the children. Here are some ideas for keeping the peace:

Kairos, *a Greek word referring to a unique time in a person's life and an opportunity for change.*

The more you can include, the more positive the results.

1. Examine your own behavior as objectively as you can to determine if you are part of the problem.

2. Create a climate of cooperation by not taking sides in the breakup.

3. Declare your desire to continue active grandparenting.

4. Demonstrate your good intentions by continued involvement.

5. Put your grandchildren's needs for positive grandparenting ahead of your own feelings by remaining neutral and supportive.

"You gotta play the hand that is dealt you. There may be pain in that hand, but you play it."

JAMES BRADY

"It's not only what happens to you that shapes your life but how you cope with it."

ANNA FREUD

If these measures fail, I highly recommend mediation as a viable alternative to arguing or going to court. You can find a mediator privately or through the court. Mediators remain neutral, using a problem-solving approach as they seek a common ground for mutual agreement. It can provide a healing experience for family members and is certainly less emotionally wrenching than going to court—and much less costly.

Mediation

"Responding to conflicts productively means utilizing the opportunities they present to change and transform the parties as human beings. It means encouraging and helping the parties to use the conflict to realize and actualize their inherent capacities both for strength of self and for relating to others."

BUSH & FOLGER, *THE PROMISE OF MEDIATION*

Mediation may be thought of as "assisted negotiation." Negotiation may be thought of as "communications for agreement." Hence, mediation is "assisted communications for agreement."

Central to mediation is the concept of "informed consent." As long as participants understand the nature of a contemplated mediation process, effectively consenting to participate in the described process, virtually any process is possible and appropriate.

The Mediation Information and Resource Center identifies seven key qualities of the mediation process:

1. **Voluntary.** You can leave at any time for any reason, or no reason.

2. **Collaborative.** You are encouraged to work together to solve your problem(s) and reach what you perceive to be your best agreement.

3. **Controlled.** You have complete decision-making power and veto power over each provision of any mediated agreement. Nothing can be imposed on you.

4. **Confidential.** Mediation is confidential, to the extent you desire and agree.

5. **Informed.** The mediation process offers a full opportunity to obtain and incorporate other expert information and advice.

6. **Impartial.** The mediator has an equal and balanced responsibility to assist each mediating party and cannot favor the interest of any one over another, nor should the mediator favor a particular result in the mediation.

7. **Self-Responsible and Satisfying.** Based upon having actively resolved your conflict, participant satisfaction, likelihood of compliance and self-esteem are found to be dramatically elevated through mediation.

A mediation usually begins with all the participants meeting together. They are guided by the mediator, trained in conflict resolution, to state their problems. This process then explores the conflicts and the obstacles, often enabling agreement where none was thought to exist.

Like in the case of Grandma Rose and Grandpa Tony. They wanted more access to their grandchildren after their son and daughter-in-law divorced. Although they seemed far apart as they sat down at the mediation table, gradually over several sessions their daughter-in-law came to realize that they were available as a support, willing to baby-sit and provide transportation and it was to her advantage to allow them greater participation in their grandchildren's lives despite her angry feelings toward her ex-husband, their son.

Mediation is much more likely to create alliances out of conflict than going to court. Mediated agreements tend to be more workable and hold up over time, with the additional advantage of reducing the emotional and financial costs.

Going to the Courts for Visitation Rights and Custody

A determined grandmother marched up to my book signing table and announced, "I saw you on television this morning and came to get your book."

Oh Lord, You don't have to move the mountain,
But give me the strength to climb

SPIRITUAL

"You must be a grandmother," I smiled. At this, tears welled in her eyes. "Yes I am, but I haven't been permitted to see little Lizzie in six months. I'm going to court next Thursday and I want the judge to see your book, *The Essential Grandparent*, because you're right. Grandparents are essential."

She proceeded to tell her story. "I used to take care of four-year-old Lizzie every weekday while her parents worked. We had such fun, a strong bond, and love each other dearly. It was great!" Then, she reported, her daughter and son-in-law's marriage ended in a bitter divorce with accusations that intimidated her daughter to relinquish custody of Lizzie to the father.

According to Grandma, Lizzie's daddy is so mean-spirited that he is refusing to let her or Grandpa see her. "So," she continued,

"We must do something ourselves, whatever we can, instead of being overwhelmed by the bad news everywhere that we become passive. Act now to wrest some positive thing out of the chaos."

MAY SARTON

"we are going to court to demand our grandparent rights. I understand that when Lizzie says she misses us, our former son-in-law tells her that 'she'll get over it.' We're heartbroken and are prepared to fight for our rights. We'll never give up. It's costing us a fortune but we are essential to that child. She needs us in her life and we need her, too." I asked Grandma Nora to keep in touch and let me know what happened.

Her letter came a few months later telling me that she did show my book to the judge. "Well," she continued, "we've been to court and the judge ordered immediate mediation, so, in essence, nothing happened except now our request for grandparent visitation with our granddaughter Lizzie is on file for the court and in the system.

"This grandparents' rights thing must be a very slow process. Now I know why grandparents don't do much when children divorce. As far as I'm concerned this stinks. It takes forever, and costs the earth. But Lizzie's worth it."

The next letter contained the good news that the grandparents had been awarded monthly visitation with Lizzie and will be sharing their daughter's month with Lizzie each summer. I await their next update.

The Custody Case of the Century

A complicated custody case and perhaps, due to its notoriety, quite possibly the "custody case of the century" is that of O.J. Simpson vs. grandparents Juditha and Lou Brown.

When their daughter, Nicole Brown Simpson, was brutally murdered, her parents (her children's grandparents) took her children from the police station on the night of the murder. Because their father, O.J. Simpson, was subsequently incarcerated, accused of the murder of their mother, the children remained with the Browns for two and one-half years.

Upon his acquittal in the murders of Nicole Brown Simpson and Ron Goldman, Simpson petitioned the court for the return of his children. After a bitter battle, a controversial and much-discussed decision by Judge Nancy Wieben Stock of the Family Court in Irvine, California, returned the children to the custody of their dad, reflecting the court's preference for the biological parent. This situation is so complex and so tragic, that it is difficult to envision a time of wholeness in these children's lives.

As a television spokesperson for grandparents, I was often asked my opinion of this custody case. My strong opposition to removing the children from their grandparents' custody was based on my knowledge of children's needs for stability and predictability. To change caretakers, schools, friends and familiar surroundings would, I reasoned, tax their already-challenged inner resources. Now that the grandparents have reopened the question of custody, I question how detrimental another change might be unless, of course, their current situation is shown to be unsatisfactory.

Variations on this theme are being repeated all across the country. Grandparents are called upon without warning or preparation to take custody of their grandchildren in a crisis. The grandparents are expected to adjust their lives to include the grandchildren, and then the grandparents must adjust again when the grandchildren leave. Because it's so emotionally and physically demanding, I recommend that grandparents raising their grandchildren join a support group.

Of course, the most important issue here is the welfare of the children. Recent studies indicate that grandchildren in the care of grandparents benefit from the attention and stability they provide.

The notion of grandparents' rights is fairly new. Many courageous and determined grandparents are fighting to define them. They are on new terrain, facing such issues as medical insurance for grandchildren in grandparents' care, financial assistance for grandparents whose custody keeps the children from becoming wards of the state in foster care, and determining permanent guardianship over the biological parents when grandparents have become a grandchild's psychological parent.

Grandparents raising their kid's kids are truly heroes.

Decisions regarding child custody should be made with the principle of the least detrimental alternative. This means that the choice should take into consideration the child's sense of time, not the adults, the opportunity to be wanted and to

85-90 percent of children in custodial care are there because of parental involvement in drugs and alcohol.

maintain a continuous relationship with at least one adult who will become the psychological parent.

Grandparents' Rights

The new concept of grandparents' rights is being tested in courts and mediation rooms across the country. Congress has recently convened a task force to begin to study the issues and the Department of Health and Human Services Administration for Children and Families has formed an Advisory Panel on Kinship Care, grandparents caring for grandchildren.

The table on pages 74 and 75 summarizes third-party visitation by state. Ninety to 95 percent of the laws governing third-party (grandparent) visitation and other grandparent rights vary from state to state. For the most up-to-date information, contact your state attorney general. [See resources for contact information.]

Grandparents are exercising their rights for access to grandchildren for visitation, and in many cases for custody, in order to rescue the children from undesirable situations. Their rights are challenged as the result of family disputes or disruption such as separation or divorce, illness, abusive behavior, incarceration and/or substance abuse (drugs or alcohol). [See resources]

According to a report by the Bureau of Justice Statistics the number of American adults imprisoned has more than doubled over the past twelve years. The United States may soon surpass Russia as the country with the highest rate of incarceration.

The number of people imprisoned in the United States has grown for more than a quarter century, helped by the increased drug prosecutions and a general get-tough policy on all classes of offenders. One out of every 150 people in the United States is behind bars. Half are for violent crimes which includes violence against women and families. One forth of those in jail are for drug offenses.

Many grandparents raising grandchildren have taken over the

TABLE SUMMARIZING THE LAW IN THE FIFTY STATES FOR THIRD-PARTY VISITATION

STATE	Step-parents	Grandparents—Death of Their Child	Grandparents—Child Divorce	Out of Wedlock	Any Interested Party
Alabama		✓	✓		
Alaska	✓	✓	✓	✓	✓
Arizona	✓1	✓	✓	✓	✓
Arkansas		✓	✓		
California	✓	✓	✓		
Colorado		✓	✓	✓	
Connecticut	✓	✓	✓	✓	✓
Delaware	✓		✓		
Dist. of Col.					
Florida		✓	✓	✓	
Georgia		✓	✓		
Hawaii	✓		✓		
Idaho			✓	✓	
Illinois		✓	✓	✓	
Indiana	✓	✓	✓	✓	
Iowa		✓	✓	✓	
Kansas	✓	✓	✓	✓	
Kentucky		✓	✓	✓	
Louisiana		✓	✓		
Maine	✓	✓	✓	✓	
Maryland		✓	✓		
Mass.		✓	✓		
Michigan	✓	✓	✓		
Minnesota	✓	✓	✓	✓	
Mississippi		✓	✓		
Missouri		✓	✓	✓	

1 New in loco parents bill allows visitation and in rare cases custody to these in loco parents.

TABLE SUMMARIZING THE LAW IN THE FIFTY STATES FOR THIRD-PARTY VISITATION

STATE	Step-parents	Grandparents—Death of Their Child	Grandparents—Child Divorce	Out of Wedlock	Any Interested Party
Montana		✓	✓	✓	
Nebraska	✓	✓	✓		
Nevada		✓	✓	✓	
New Hamp.	✓	✓	✓	✓	
New Jersey	✓	✓	✓	✓	
New Mexico	✓	✓	✓	✓	✓
New York	✓	✓	✓	✓	
N. Carolina			✓		
North Dakota	✓	✓	✓		✓
Ohio	✓	✓	✓	✓	✓2
Oklahoma		✓	✓	✓	
Oregon	✓	✓	✓	✓	✓
Pennsylvania		✓	✓		
Rhode Island		✓	✓		
S. Carolina		✓	✓	✓	
South Dakota		✓	✓	✓	
Tennessee	✓		✓		
Texas	✓	✓	✓	✓	✓
Utah	✓	✓	✓	✓	✓
Vermont		✓	✓		
Virginia					✓3
Washington	✓		✓		
West Virginia		✓	✓	✓	
Wisconsin		✓	✓		
Wyoming	✓	✓	✓		✓

2 Extends only to relatives of minor child.

3 This, of course, includes any relative of a step-parent.

parental role because their children's marriages dissolved as a result of abuse, drugs and/or incarceration. We need to address the underlying social problems represented by these numbers. We must make a commitment to policies that strengthen families so that they can provide the stability and the glue that holds families together.

Eighty percent of women who enter prisons have a history of drug abuse. Programs that address recovery in prison with care and an after-care component have proven to be effective. So many of these incarcerated women are mothers, and even grandmothers, who return to their communities with visitation rights or regained custody of their children and/or grandchildren. Without intervention while incarcerated they are doomed to repeat their offenses and return to jail, a perennial revolving door.

California has a model program with a 90 percent succes rate. "Forever Free" is a program that begins recovery from substance abuse in prison. *The State of California took nine months of my life but gave me my life,* stated one successful graduate of this program. *Our children need us to be mothers again,* said another who is still undergoing rehabilitation. As a part of these programs, mothers and grandmothers are being taught parenting skills along with social, career and leisure time skills. One program uses my book, *The Essential Grandparent: A Guide To Making A Difference,* to help grandmothers who look forward to returning to their families.

According to the latest census figures 3.9 million children in the United States are being raised by grandparents. This number increased 40 percent between 1993 and 1996 primarily due to substance abuse.

3.9 million grandchildren are being raised by grandparents in 2.5 million households

1.3 million are grandparent couples

1.1 million are single grandmothers

157,000 are single grandfathers

Of these 3.9 million children:

> Two-thirds are living in three generation households (grandparent and at least one parent, who could be a teenager)

> One-third is in grandparent only households (no middle generation)

Grandparents raising grandchildren are truly heroes. They have put aside their own hopes and dreams to parent young children once again, and at a time in their lives when their own health and finances are on the wane. They need help to find and negotiate their way through the maze of agencies that might supply relief. We need to create new social supports and delivery systems for these "GrandFamilies" who are keeping their families together despite hardships.

"The very basis of the family has changed," concludes a demographic report issued in 1994 by the fifteen European Union countries. "The family that in the past was an institution and means of social integration has become a pact between two individuals looking for personal fulfillment."
LOS ANGELES TIMES,
JULY 18, 1995

When grandparents must take over, they often experience a sense of failure, believing that their own imperfect parenting makes them responsible for the problems. Financial hardships bear down on these grandparents, forcing them to reduce their time at work and requiring them to stretch their often-limited retirement incomes. Unfortunately, grandparents who have taken over the care of grandchildren are not eligible for financial grants or aid as foster parents, although they are serving in that capacity. Many grandparents who have found themselves in this boat are fighting for legislation

General Colin Powell's America's Promise has identified five promises that children need to be successful in life. The Number One promise is to have a caring adult, one who believes in the them. Often that caring adult who is making the difference is a grandparent.

that would recognize their situation by providing the relief of financial aid. [See resources.]

Single Parenting

Although most often the result of divorce, there are more lifestyle options being exercised today and many circumstances that lead to single parenting. Whatever the reason, single parents and their children need grandparent support.

For the approximately 30 percent of American households consisting of single adults with kids, it is an unmapped road that can lead right off an emotional cliff. They've found out the hard way that they can't have it all. Something's got to give. It's a juggling act between children, career and social life. If the children are the first priority, the social life is first to suffer. This results in social isolation and loneliness. Single parents are in need of your love and whatever else you can give.

"I'm so busy and so tired—and utterly without options—that I can't bother to think about my social life. My children come first."
SINGLE FATHER OF TWO

No one has answers to the tough dilemmas of single parents. Grandparents have their work cut out for them. One of the problems is that the single parent's needs are so great, grandparents find themselves feeling guilty that they're not doing enough. It is important for a grandparent to recognize that, as much as you might like to, you can't make it all better. The best you can do is the best you can do.

Build your relationship with your grandchildren so that they can accept the emotional support and the sense of family you provide. Everything you do is important: any financial support, large or small, such as special treats for children or parent; providing relief by taking care of the children by sitting, carpooling, cooking or doing some errands or chores; and lending positive encouragement all make a difference.

You can almost feel the single-parent struggle expressed in the poetry of a mother with two teenage daughters. This soft-spoken, fortyish artist, who works in an office by day, tells her story of broken dreams and the challenge of raising teenagers.

THE CONTEMPORARY FAMILY
(IT'S A CLASSIC PLIGHT)

There are three of them now,
Mother and two daughters
One, golden with light—
One dark with keen sight;
and father has long since gone.

The mother does what she can.
There's such struggle to keep unity.
It seems a classic plight;
A challenge of the century.

ANNE NORBERG

Often related to divorce are problems about getting to see the grandchildren. When access becomes an issue, grandparents are understandably upset. Many grandparents are deprived of contact with grandchildren because the custodial parent, usually not their own child, won't allow them to visit. Due to the recognition of the importance of the grandparent-grandchild relationship, there is legal recourse in many states. Of course, a day in court does not automatically win the case, and legal action creates such expense and emotional turmoil that it should be a last resort. Consider the alternative of mediation.

An Innovative Housing Solution

Here is a model for communities to follow, an innovative program for support of GrandFamilies, grandparent-headed households. Boston Aging Concerns-Young and Old United (BAC-YOU) has recently renovated an abandoned nursing home to create twenty-six apartments for grandparents raising grandchildren. There is a director living on the premises and a built-in support system for both the grandparents and the children with exercise and health programs, transportation, baby-sitting, tutoring and after school activities. It is an elegant solution that serves the many needs of these families and deserves to be studied and replicated because it is literally saving lives. The funding comes from federal (HUD), state and private sources. It represents an innovative architectural solution for recycling old buildings.

8

When Grandparents Divorce

The median age of divorced people is about fifty, and 58 percent are women.

The 50 percent divorce rate in this country is impacting older Americans as well. The number of couples seeking new alternatives and more interesting lives through divorce in their fifties and later is on the rise. Divorce among grandparents is a growing phenomenon.

How does a marriage collapse after holding together for twenty, thirty or forty years? We assume that a long marriage means you've worked out the kinks. Well, as the song goes, *It ain't necessarily so.* There are no easy answers to explain Grandma and Grandpa's divorce. What we do know is that, *According to the 1990 census, 6.2 percent of Americans sixty years old and older were divorced.* when it happens, it sends shock waves throughout the family.

As we seek understanding, it is evident that each story is individual, unique to its participants. However, some identifiable trends are contributing to this growing trend of elder divorce.

Longevity

Grandparents have changed. We're younger due to health and lifestyle and older because we're living longer. Percentagewise, the fastest-growing segment of our population is that of centenarians (people over the age of one hundred). Today a person in his fifties or sixties can reasonably expect to live another twenty to thirty years or more.

This lengthened life span presents older Americans, grandparents, with many challenges. What are we going to do with these added years? What will provide the most fulfillment? What is most meaningful? A longer life span encourages change, and sometimes that change spells separation or divorce.

Ed and Sheila, both in their late fifties with successful careers, had been struggling with their marriage for many years. Sheila felt suffocated in the relationship and suffered with depression. In her view, they had little in common outside of their shared interest in three grown children and three grandchildren. Despite their mutual respect, they experienced a repetitive cycle of positive resolve to make it work, which gradually deteriorated, giving way to Sheila's angry outbursts and Ed's passive-aggressive response. After hitting bottom they would regroup with new resolve, only to begin the cycle again.

In the United States, the average age to become a grandparent (the birth of the first grandchild) is forty-seven years. Seventy-two percent of all Americans over fifty (60 million people) are grandparents. This number is projected to increase 20 percent in the next ten years.

Finally they decided to divorce. Selling the family house, dividing their assets and beginning new lives undermined their security and was devastating. "We suffered an enormous sense of loss, sadness and lack of stability," Sheila told me. "During the first year I wondered if I would survive the change." Ed was hurt and puzzled and had to work at accepting that the divorce was not a sign of personal failure.

Their kids did their best to be supportive, but it was a great loss for them as well. They lost their family home and, although they visit their parents separately, it's not the same. *They can't go home again.*

Sheila told me how the grandchildren were also affected. "When we visited the grandchildren at Christmas, the eldest who was six years old, asked, 'Grandmommy, don't you love Granddaddy any more?' I answered, 'Yes, I do love him but it's better for us to live in separate houses.' He pondered this and then shrugged, 'I guess you just like to be lonesome.' It broke my heart.

"Well, now almost three years later, we've survived and agree life is good, but still challenging. Living alone is lonely. The family remains our priority. Recently we cohosted our daughter's wedding, and it was really a warm, family event. We are both active grandparents; those little ones mean everything."

> *"I don't want to live out my life with this repeating pattern of anger and remorse in our relationship."*
>
> SIXTY-ONE-YEAR-OLD DIVORCEE, AFTER THIRTY-FIVE YEARS OF MARRIAGE

Empty Nest Syndrome

"We stayed together for the kids." Sometimes the children are the glue that holds a marriage together. When the kids leave home, the parents are confronted with each other. Some couples discover that there's nothing left to hold them together. Others find that when they come face to face, without the children as distractions, they can't tolerate the habits or attitudes that have aggravated them over the years and decide it's time to split.

A child's presence may provide a buffer between the partners and their marital difficulties, especially when there has been verbal or physical abuse, alcoholism, mental illness, chronic financial problems or personality clashes throughout the marriage. The empty nest dissolves the buffer children provide, and the frustrations and anger are no longer contained.

> *A more positive view of the current divorce rate is that it is a result of social change rather than a cause. Families are trying to survive and evolve within a rapidly changing society.*

The "Peggy Lee Syndrome"

Remember the lyrics to that haunting Peggy Lee song: "Is That All There Is?" As you begin to number your days, you also begin to look back over your life and question, "Is that all there is and then you're gone?" Such an assessment can create a certain urgency to make sure we don't miss out on what life has to offer. Some people actually panic at this thought. They feel that they have somehow missed out and, in an effort to counteract the panic, they may be propelled to seek more. This attempt to seek more causes them to discard the old and look for new adventures and new partners.

> *"I was twelve years old when my grandparents divorced. Although my grandfather was an alcoholic, he was my hero. My parents sided with my grandmother, and I lost my hero. It was devastating and now, at forty-six years old, I still suffer the loss."*
> RADIO TALK-SHOW HOST

Male Menopause

Dr. Mark Blackman, chief of endocrinology and metabolism at Johns Hopkins Bayview Medical Center, believes *male menopause* is a real phenomenon. He estimates that more than 25 million men in the United States are currently experiencing symptoms of male menopause, which include depression, anxiety and reduced sexual function.

> *"We will be judged by the same judgment we use."*

Fifty-two percent of men between the ages of forty and seventy suffer from some degree of erectile dysfunction. Their reduced libido is accompanied by an increasing desire to prove that they can still perform. This pushes many men to seek new partners, multiple partners and often a younger partner to enhance their feeling of youth. The result is that they leave their older wives.

Renewed male potency due to Viagra may be restoring men's sexual abilities and enhancing marriages but it is evidently having some unexpected side effects. While enjoying renewed vigor, some men have begun to question their marriages and look for greener pastures.

Tina was in a complete state of shock when her husband of over thirty years told her he planned a divorce. She claims she hadn't a clue that this was coming but now, years later, she chalks this up to major denial. It was such a blow. Without warning she lost her comfortable and safe life. Despondent, she despaired and suffered severe depression. Time has given her a more philosophic view of her husband's betrayal (yes, there was another woman). Today her new life includes a male companion, family and friends and travels. But she has not been left unscarred.

"Viagra helped my husband. It was great but, now, after thirty years of marriage, he's not sure he wants to be married anymore. Viagra affects the brain as well as what's below the belt."

Another story, told by a thirty-six-year-old daughter, has an unexpected twist. Grandmother's heartbreak has ultimately led her to a new role as caretaker of her grandchildren, which has become an invaluable gift to the family.

"Three years ago I had to rush to my mother's side in another state. She had collapsed and was rushed to the hospital after my Dad told her that, after thirty-five years, he no longer wanted to be married. Mother just wanted to die. Although only fifty-three years old, she was ready to give up.

"I had no choice but to move her in with me. She needed to be nourished back to life or she would have gone into a corner and wasted away. Fortunately my husband was very accepting.

"It's funny how things work out in life. At the time that Mother moved in, our only child was our fourteen-year-old son. Our wish for more children was never granted. Shortly after Mom came to live with us, my sister, Lisa, was diagnosed with a terminal illness. Lisa had three children, two boys and a girl. Because of Lisa's poor health, the youngest, a one-year-old boy, came to live with me and Mom was there to help out. When my sister died, her other son joined our family. So we now have the family we had wished for: two boys, four and five years old, plus our seventeen-year-old son. My other sister took our little niece. While my husband and I work full-time, Mom runs the household. She cooks and cleans and looks after her three grandsons.

"We're raising three boys now and, looking back, marvel at what seems to us a plan. Here we are with my Mom, our son, and our two nephews as a functioning family unit while nearby my sister with her two daughters and niece make up our extended family. We are close and supportive. It's a busy life and I must admit I get weary of the relentless responsibilities but take comfort in the joyful fact that *we are a family* and Mom's got a clear purpose in life and is even beginning to get out and about again."

The Lingering Effects of Divorce

Divorce is never final. Whenever it takes place, the impact on a family continues for a lifetime. My auto mechanic was telling me his story of early divorce and of its lingering effects into grandparenthood.

"I was divorced when my two children were small." Nat sounded resigned. As he continued his story it was obvious that he had suffered a lifetime of frustration. "I disagreed with my wife. We never saw eye to eye. Recently, my grown daughter moved away to a neighboring state with her husband and her children, our grandchildren. My ex-wife followed her. She lives near our daughter, gives her money and encourages what I view as an irresponsible lifestyle. I can't compete. It sure gets in the way of seeing and spending time with my grandchildren. My ex has effectively divided the family.

"Our son, on the other hand, still lives nearby, is not under mother's thumb and we have a good father-son relationship. I am grateful to at least have him."

Single Grandparenting

"It's lonely being a single grandparent. When I plan and serve a family dinner I am reminded that I'm alone. I can't help thinking of the images on television of Grandma and Grandpa greeting the family, of Grandpa carving the turkey. It's so warm.

Now that I'm alone I have to generate the whole thing. Of course, I'm grateful to have the family around but it's not the way I imagined growing old."

Of course, single grandparenthood comes not only from divorce but from death and sometimes illness as well. A single grandparent is required to carry on the role, impart traditions and provide for family solidarity without the expected support of a spouse.

How can you keep your spirits up?

- Refuse to feel sorry for yourself. Remember, you're not the only one in your predicament and you still have family.

- Keep your thoughts on the goal of having a warm family gathering.

- Ask others to help. Join forces with friends and other families.

- You are still the head the family. They rely on you to model a good life.

- Fulfill your grandparent role to provide unconditional love, continuity, security and stability.

- Your attitude shapes your life.

An Outing

These stories vary but they have one thing in common. The heartbreak of divorce later in life provokes a particular sadness and fear. Sadness over the thoughts of wasted years and the fears of starting over at a time when aging is an issue and the thought of starting over alone provokes terror. It is daunting.

"It took me several years to deal with the rage I had for my former husband. I knew there was something wrong in our marriage and pleaded to go to couples therapy. He refused, but finally the truth came out. Stan was concealing his homosexuality. I could have accepted that, but when he admitted picking up men and having unprotected sex while we continued to have sexual relations, I went ballistic.

"I couldn't believe that, after all these years, he would have so little regard for me. He exposed me to AIDS! I joined an AIDS support group—me a middle class grandmother who worked in an art gallery. Can you imagine! I would never have dreamt in a million years that I would become a candidate for that dread disease.

"It was humiliating. I moved away from our community and even changed my name. I'm lucky to be healthy. I've gradually picked up the pieces to create a new life. It's been hard on our son, who does stay in touch with his dad. Fortunately, our little grandson is too young to understand. We'll have to face that one down the road. But, for now, I'm doing okay and hope that maybe, someday, I'll regain my trust in people."

The shock of discovery that a person you've known for many years is not the person you thought they were rocks one's foundation and causes a reordering of perceptions. How can a person keep from letting it embitter their life? These stories demonstrate that it takes time, prayer and a willingness to work it through.

Now that Betty is single, she is working as a home health-care provider. "It takes so little to make people happy," she reported. "When they say, 'Oh, that looks nice,' or 'You're so thoughtful,' it makes me feel needed again since my kids are grown and tend to ignore me.

"I'm in the midst of divorce after thirty-six years of marriage. The day before my birthday, Ed left for his brother's in Texas. I was surprised. Then he went to live with our son. I was angry because he didn't deserve to be with the grandkids and he put them in the middle. 'Tell Grandma. . . .' Four-year-old Brianna, who lives nearby, didn't understand. Papa was gone and wasn't coming back. 'I miss Papa,' she told me. 'I do, too,' I answered honestly.

"I've had the hardest time with my youngest daughter, who was always Daddy's girl. When I was telling her that Dad ran away from financial problems, she said, 'Don't talk to me about my father.' Finally she went to counseling and was able to say, 'Mama, I'm glad you're here.'

"Jim was a good father and we were always a close family. Jim and I didn't have advantages growing up and we tried to make a better home for ourselves and our kids. Maybe that's why we stayed together so long. But the communication's not there.

"I just arranged a family conference call with my counselor, three kids, my son-in-law and daughter-in-law. This was a major step. We're not known for talking, which is part of what was wrong with our marriage. I'm by myself and I need more contact with my kids. My oldest son is gay and single and we have wonderful talks. My younger son is in the computer field and it's like a business call when we talk. I was thrilled that they were all willing to participate and everyone talked. It has made me feel much better and not so alone.

I was fed up. I didn't want to live out my final years with conflict.

GRANDFATHER AFTER THIRTY-TWO YEARS OF MARRIAGE

"I've been very angry. I don't want to run into him, and I realize I sound like a bitch when I talk to him. But I have to be civil because of the kids and grandkids. I'm really involved with the grandkids. I'll drive three hundred miles to be there for the first day of school. They are my joy."

Changes and Challenges When Grandparents Divorce

Developmental stages continue throughout life. We're never grown up, once and for all. *Development is not over 'til it's over.* Change is the law of nature. As we age, we face continuous losses: our energy, our bodies, our family and friends. And we have to keep getting reacquainted with that older person who is looking back at us in the mirror. We must seek courage to keep going with enthusiasm, to continue to grow and seek the wonder of the world. Too often this aging process is experienced silently.

BREAK THE MIRROR

In the morning
After taking cold shower
―――――――――*what a mistake*―――――――――
I look at the mirror.

There, a funny guy,
Gray hair, white beard, wrinkled skin,
―――――*what a pity*―――――
Poor, dirty, old man!
He is not me, absolutely not.

Land and life
Fishing in the ocean
Sleeping in the desert with stars
Building a shelter in mountains
Farming the ancient way
Singing with coyotes
Singing against nuclear war—
I'll never be tired of life.
Now I'm seventeen years old,
Very charming young man.
I sit down quietly in lotus position,
Meditating, meditating for nothing.
Suddenly a voice comes to me:

> *"To stay young,*
> *To save the world,*
> *Break the mirror."*

NANAO SAKAKI

What Grandparents Experience
When They Divorce

These are the issues for grandparents and families as they face the new experiences that accompany divorce.

Enormous Sense of Loss

The loss of security, of structure and purpose creates confusion. *"The first year was horrible. So much sadness."* Some of the issues facing divorcing grandparents are similar to those faced by a grandparent when a spouse dies.

When contemplating a divorce after twenty-seven years of marriage, fifty-six-year-old Fran said, "We couldn't work as a team. The intensity of the pain was unbearable."

Then Some Relief and Renewal

The absence of tension and stress from the relationship is a relief. *"I feel liberated and autonomous,"* exclaimed one grandmother. Happier grandparents are better grandparents and role models.

Need to Learn New Tasks

Typically marriages have some division of labor. Husbands and wives each assume certain tasks from taking out the trash, marketing or managing social obligations to car repairs, bill paying and financial management. Divorce forces each partner to learn to do things they may never have done.

Men: Traditionally men have little experience with cooking, running a household or meeting social obligations.

Women: must take over financial responsibilities and deal with house and car maintenance. Women also face safety issues when going out at night or traveling alone.

SINGLE SLICES By Peter Kohlsaat

Single Slices by Peter Kohlsaat.
©1999 *Los Angeles Times* Syndicate. Reprinted by permission.

Financial Issues

Financial problems create a special challenge at a time when it's not as easy to make more money. A reduced standard of living is never easy and furthers the sense of loss and security. Social Security and Medicare provide a safety net and are social supports for the older person.

New Social Roles

Divorce causes social upheaval. It is isolating. Friends and relatives react to divorce in surprising ways. Some are threatened and withdraw while others are angry. Some side with one or the other partner. Divorce requires a new plan for a new way of life.

Stability of a Family Place Is Threatened

Suddenly the grandparents feel homeless and saddened by the recognition that home will never be the same. It is a loss of place.

"My grandparent's house was part of my compass, there's North, South, East, West and Gram and Gramps."
FORTY-YEAR-OLD GRANDDAUGHTER

What Families Experience When Grandparents Divorce

Grandchildren feel threatened and are often confused. They personalize their grandparents' divorce and worry that their parents will also divorce. They experience the loss of the family solidarity.

Parent-adult child relationships can rupture. The kids may take sides, unable to handle the stress, embarrassed (especially if there's a third party involved) or critical of their parents. Even as adults, hearing about your own parent's sexuality, Dad's young girl friend or Mom's affair is uncomfortable.

I'm glad you're just separated from Grandpa and not divorced. Being divorced is much worse than being separated.
FIVE-YEAR-OLD GRANDSON

Adult children often feel cheated of the family stability on which they depend. This may revive early childhood fears of loss or abandonment. Parental divorce causes a reevaluation of an adult child's perceptions of their family, both past and present. They worry about their own marriages as their symbol of family solidarity crumbles. This triggers a role reversal with a new sense of responsibility for the welfare of their parents.

Stability of a family place is threatened. Suddenly grandchildren and adult children feel homeless. *You can't go home again*; home will never be the same.

Holidays and celebrations will never be the same. Family togetherness becomes a broken dream, especially when the grandparents are at odds. One grandmother refused to be at the same event as the grandfather and his new wife, creating a deeper split in the family. When a single grandparent hosts Thanksgiving dinner it revives old memories, sadness and anger.

Adjustments must be made to new spouses and extended families. Among the feelings that arise from these adjustments are incompatibility, jealousies and concerns about inheritance.

Guidelines for Grandparents

How to Tell the Kids?

Consider together how you will tell the children and grandchildren. Assess how much of a shock this will be. Is it more comfortable to tell them together or separately?

- Talk to them without burdening them with your troubles.
- Reassure your grandchildren that you will still be there for them. This doesn't mean that their own parents will divorce.
- Continue to do things together.

Don't Be Divisive

Don't be divisive by talking against your spouse. It further weakens the family. No matter how you feel. You are always your child's mother or father. Although children see parents in a more realistic light as they grow up, they still need us. Parental divorce, no matter what your stage of life, can be painful.

Avoid putting your kids in the middle by refusing to be at the same gathering as your ex or by talking to each other through the children. Such behavior adds to a sense of loss and stress and pulls the kids into your problems. Their discomfort can result in their staying away.

Keeping the Family Together

Resolve that a family with children remains a family. No matter what shape or size you become with extended or blended families, maintain the family ties.

It is important to appreciate that families who are able to recover from the pain and disappointment of divorce can indeed be healthy and happy families again.

Plan Time for Your Family

Plan time with your family, especially with the grandchildren. They need you. Being involved with them can provide solace and nourishment for us. Continue to plan and participate in holiday events but don't expect your family and grandchildren to provide a life for you.

Maintain a Positive Attitude

Recognize that transitions are always challenging and that things do get better. Choose to make each day the best day it can be. Continue to be a positive role model.

Seek Outside Help

Don't hesitate to seek support from a counselor, minister or support group. Reduce your sense of isolation by getting involved in something outside of yourself, like work or a hobby. Even better, be of service by volunteering to help others. When we give to others we also give to ourselves. Every community has many opportunities. Become a mentor, take care of a grandchild. Grandpa Dan volunteered as a mentor at the local elementary school. *"It changed my life!"*

Remember that Grandparenting Well Is a Key to Aging Well

Reading to my grandchildren, running down a hill with my granddaughter, sharing the excitement of taking apart a telephone with a six-year-old to see how it's made . . . these positive experiences actually strengthen the immune system.

Remember: Our children inherit not only the legacy that their elders impart but also the void that is left by what they withhold. Grandparents, regardless of your circumstances, never doubt it: *You are essential!*

"The Times, They Are A-Changing . . ."

After thirty-three years of marriage, Vera Goldman filed for divorce. She and her husband had amassed a large fortune. Under New York law, women are usually given "equitable distribution" of the total assets at the discretion of the judge (usually a small percentage of the total).

Mrs. Goldman sued her husband and fought for equal, not equitable, distribution. She won this precedent-setting 1998 case and received half of their total wealth of $44 million.

Sitting in her new sports car she smiled, "When you reach your sixties you're in the third act. I consider divorce my retirement."

"There is only one solution if old age is not to be an absurd parody of our former life, and that is to go on pursuing ends that give our existence meaning—devotion to individuals, to groups or causes, social, political, intellectual or creative work. . . . One's life has value as long as one attributes value to the life of others, by means of love, friendship, indignation, compassion."

SIMONE DE BEAUVOIR

Hope

As divorce liberates from a history of conflict, a shared love of the family emerges. It holds the healing faith that what they hold sacred will endure. Their journey continues. . . .

SINGLE SLICES By Peter Kohlsaat

9

Who's Coming for the Holidays?

The New Blended and Extended Family

Blend: *to mix, mingle, inter-mix; a mixture formed by blending various sorts or qualities, with some coloring from the other sources. To mix intimately or harmoniously so that their individuality is obscured in the product.*

Extend: *to stretch or pull out to its full size; to lengthen; to prolong in duration; to widen in range or scope.*

Result: *Us, the Ex, the Ex's new mate, the new mate's Ex, and the Kids.*

Definitions are neutral, open to your interpretation. The notion of a new blended or extended family challenges preconceived expectations and our adaptability to change.

Divorce may be an ending but it is also a beginning, the beginning of a new life for the divorced couple, each going their own way but tied together forever by their children. New relationships bring new friends to the family. These new friends who may ultimately become new family members change the family's dynamics once again. Divorce is a new beginning for the family.

**Why Einstein quickly moved on to
general relativity.**

Were you ever a new kid in the classroom? Do you remember when a new kid arrived in your school? A newcomer precipitates a change in the social order that reverberates through the classroom. Some find it threatening and automatically close the person out. Others may cautiously attend to the newcomer and a few may extend themselves warmly. Well, families react similarly because introducing a newcomer creates disequilibrium in a family's social structure.

Eighty percent of divorced people remarry.

After a divorce, grandparents and parents must expect the inevitability of welcoming newcomers to the fold. A new friend or spouse may arrive with their own kids, as well. This is really getting complicated!

> After a holiday dinner at the home of my ex-husband and his wife, my husband exclaimed, "It's so good to have family!" It had been a delightfully relaxed evening. This blended family included the second wife's grandchild and her grandchild's stepsister; our daughter, son-in-law and granddaughter; and the daughter of our son's fiancée. The kids got along, the adults shared good conversation and we felt it was an accomplishment. Wow!

One possible beneficial result is that divorces expand the family circle. "That's certainly true of ours," reports President Jimmy Carter in his book *The Virtues of Aging.* "Two of our sons remarried, so we have two extra families. And at a recent family reunion I noticed that one of my cousins had three daughters with nine husbands among them—and only one is still married."

Don't have me at the same event with my ex.

Kids can't get too much love.

> *The extended family is in our lives again. This should make all the people happy who were complaining back in the sixties and seventies that the reason family life was so hard, especially on mothers, was that the nuclear family has replaced the extended family. . . . Your basic extended family today includes your ex-husband or -wife, your ex's new mate, your new mate, possibly your new mate's ex, and any new mate that your new mate's ex has acquired. It consists entirely of people who are not related by blood, many of whom can't stand each other. This return of the extended family reminds me of the favorite saying of my friend's extremely pessimistic mother: Be careful what you wish for, you might get it.*
>
> DELIA EPHRON, *FUNNY SAUCE*

Embracing Togetherness

Here's a model for inclusiveness that achieved its goal of a joyful celebration. This is applicable for any type of gathering, large or small, weddings, birthdays or any time the blended and extended get together.

While planning the hotel luncheon for son Gary's bar mitzvah, the former and current wife suddenly had the chilling vision of a room filled with guests divided into two armed camps. "You know, my ex's family and friends on one side and mine on the other," said the ex-wife. That would be deadly so we decided to mix it up. To set the tone, all the parents and grandparents sat together at one table and each table was made up of guests from both sides.

People who must carry their own water and build their house of sticks but have an extended family are enviable.
JASON CARTER, PEACE CORPS, SOUTH AFRICA

That also solved the problem of how to seat mutual friends. It worked! It was a warm occasion, filled with happiness and pride as the guests were immediately put at ease by the obvious camaraderie in the family.

Instant Grandparenting: Remarriage and Other Surprises

Instant grandparenting results from of a variety of situations. For whatever reason it occurs, remarriage (your kids or your own), *Toujours l'amour. The French call step-fathers "beau-pere," or beautiful father.* adoption or other events, it is an unexpected gift and challenge. Three key factors determine your relationship to your step-grandchild:

1. *The age of the step-grandchild upon entering your life.* The younger the age of the step-child when you meet, the greater the chance that you will be readily accepted and have the possibility for a close relationship. Older children are less available since they are busy with school work, friends and activities.

2. *Who the step-grandchild lives with full-time.* If the child is in the custodial care of a parent you have a relationship with, then naturally you will have more access and encouragement to develop your own relationship than if the child lives outside the extended family.

3. *How you feel about it.* Whether you find the step-grandchild appealing and want to devote your time to being a grandparent is a very personal decision. It requires time for this notion of step-grandparenting to grow on you. It is possible that you just don't feel comfortable with the child, parents or situation.

Most parents will welcome your involvement if you ask their permission and demonstrate your good intentions. Grandparenting step-grandchildren can be successful, but not if you pretend that they are just like biological grandchildren. You must first become friends. When you are able to open your heart and give of yourself, rewards follow.

New Lifestyles

Sandy and Robert sounded quite amazed as they announced they were becoming grandparents. "What's so surprising about becoming grandparents?" I asked. "Well, we didn't expect it because none of our children are married." It turns out that their son's longtime girlfriend was expecting his baby. The prospective parents had no plans to live together although their son was accepting his role as father. "We feel we're being cheated," complained the prospective grandparents. They felt a complicated mix of feelings: anger, embarrassment and excitement.

Then Sandy made this wistful statement. "I've wished for years that I would have something nice to put in the Church bulletin . . . an engagement, a wedding, a grandchild . . . and now we're becoming grandparents and I can't even announce it." Then she added "My parents were very conservative people, they'd be turning over in their graves if they knew."

"How do you see your role as grandparents?" I asked. "We just want to love this grandchild," they agreed. The child has arrived, a girl. They flew up to see her and were thrilled. They don't enjoy easy access to the child.

There's some dissension between the other grandmother and their son. But, the new grandbaby along with her mother and father attended Sandy and Bob's anniversary party.

Now, several years later, the parents of their granddaughter are estranged. It wasn't a marriage and now it's not a divorce but Sandy and Bob are determined to participate in this little girl's life. They're just not sure how. . . .

Grandma Janet is struggling with her daughter's new lifestyle. Obviously agitated, she began to tell me her story at my booksigning. Her daughter is divorcing a loving and kind husband. "I love my son-in-law and I can't believe what my daughter has done," she continued. "My daughter has taken up with another woman and a most unpleasant one at that. Her husband was patient and tried to be accepting but after two years decided 'I can't continue to live like this.' I just can't get over my anger and disgust at this whole mess my daughter has created. And I worry about my two granddaughters."

This grandmother's rage is, most likely, masking her shock and distress by this revelation of her daughter's sexual preference. It may also be covering deep-seated, unconscious concerns regarding her own sexual preference. Her own manner appeared rather masculine, which may be an expression of ambivalence regarding her own sexual orientation, and, in turn, would make her daughter's choice personally threatening. Not a simple matter.

Our children's choices and lifestyles may not be easy to accept. Support groups can help. When you find yourself in a situation that stirs up strong reactions, seek some counseling for a healthy solution. For example, Grandma Janet's attitude is important to her granddaughters and will influence their understanding and ability to process this profound change. Resolving her feelings will benefit others in the family.

Sometimes, the differences that cause distress are due to religion, race, culture or even age. As social barriers are lowered interracial, interreligious and intercultural unions are becoming more common.

Two women who attended my class on grandparenting were a couple. They proudly announced they were about to become grandparents and were taking my course to celebrate and prepare for their new role. Gail's daughter was about to have her first child. "And how will you both be accepted as grandparents of this new baby?" I asked.

As a committed couple for many years they enjoy a good relationship with the mother-to-be and her husband who welcome their care and support. A heartwarming story of the acceptance of difference. This new baby will be surrounded by love.

In California the most popular name for a boy has been Michael or John. This year, the most popular name for a boy is José, reflecting the change in population due to immigration from south of the border.

Between a Rock and a Hard Place

Families' hold strong notions about taking sides in a divorce—notions which may be overt or subtle. Grandma Della was surprised to discover that, many years after her son's divorce, he felt betrayed by her continuing relationship with Nancy, his former wife and the mother of her grandson. Tom is a very reasonable sort, a physician whose divorce was fairly amicable. He has not outwardly harbored anger toward Nancy and it seemed natural that Grandma Della and the rest of the family maintain their relationships.

Tom's sister chimed in that she was eager for the cousins, her son and her brother's son, to continue their relationship, as well. Now, more than twelve years later, Tom is admitting he feels betrayed by his family's friendship with his ex-wife. It has saddened the family. Grandma commented that, even if she had known, she would have continued her relationship with Nancy over Tom's objections because of her

The point of life is to make mistakes. As long as you're making mistakes you're okay. Just don't make the same mistakes.

grandson. But Tom's sister expressed some reservations. She is sorry she has unknowingly hurt her brother's feelings but, on the other hand, happy that the two cousins are friends.

Family members may be less accepting of continued relationships than the divorced couple. Sara told me that when her ex-husband attended her mother's funeral she felt it was a fitting tribute to their genuine relationship. "He appreciated Mom and what she did as a grandparent but my sister was quite put out about his presence. When she turned to me and snapped 'What's he doing here?' I didn't understand why she felt he didn't belong. After all, she was the grandmother of his kids." Some family members may feel they are showing loyalty to the divorced member of their family or that somehow they were personally rejected by the in-law. It could be a case of misplaced anger. Whatever it is, and no matter how justified one feels about it, these attitudes serve to further divide the family and provide another dimension of deprivation and loss for the children of divorce.

"My sister-in-law and I had a close relationship," reported Grandma Ellie. "In fact, I met my husband through her. When we announced our divorce I know she was shocked and felt protective of her brother. It was a personal loss when she not only refused to continue contact with me but kept the cousins apart. I heard that she felt our children were now from an unstable home and she needed to protect her children from them. It sounds outlandish to me but there was no reasoning here. It was over. The kids were the biggest losers. To their credit, my in-laws remained interested grandparents and remained above the fray. Now, many years later, we are all grandparents and the tide has turned. The cousins are in touch with each other and I have enjoyed some nice talks with my former sister-in-law. Better late than never."

Joy Shared Is Multiplied, Problems Shared Are Divided

John and Peggy continue a friendly relationship which serves as a comfort for both of them. They have been divorced for almost twenty-five years and John is remarried. Issues about their three children, most particularly their mentally retarded adult daughter's care, require their collaboration. They have a good working relationship and despite differences provide support for their daughter. John's current wife joins with them at times. *We're all in this together* is her motto.

"Enjoying our grandchildren together really feels good," Grandma Phyllis announced. "Our new partners join in, too. It's been many years since our divorce and we have all mellowed. What we treasure is family and the thrill of seeing these little ones grow. Oh, I admit, sometimes I am reminded of why we divorced and, at times, feel a bit jealous when my ex and his wife are doing something really great with the grandchildren—something I wish I was doing it with them. But I quickly remind myself how fortunate it is for the grandchildren to have these experiences. Life is too short to have it any other way."

Sometimes, the best help we offer is to just be there to listen.

Tips for Enhancing Your Blended and Extended Family

- Be thoughtful. Ask the new wife about her family.
- Remember new family members at birthdays and special occasions.
- Remember former family members (ex-sisters-in-law), too.
- Include former family members in family reunions whenever possible.
- Reach out. Meet people more than half way.
- Be open. Be wary of preconceived notions and prejudices.
- Establish individual relationships within your families.
- Honor the culture and tradition of others. Ask them to bring food, music and stories to share.
- Assist children's relationships with planned activities. An art table, games, a project can get them together.
- Plan activities for participation by all.
- Singing, word games, going around the table and telling what they're thankful for brings people together.
- Introducing people with warmth and a smile sets the tone at family gatherings.
- Don't make comparisons between children of any age. It promotes jealousy.
- Focus on your goal to create a family. Overlook the small stuff.
- Never forget your sense of humor.
- Blended and extended families work when their members have a positive attitude.

Epilogue

Two Generations

*We look at the world, You and I
And what do we see?
I as the world once was—and you
As it might be.*

Martin Buxbaum

Ask yourself: Who in my life has helped me love the good that is in me? Who in my life has loved me and wanted the best for me? Take a few moments to think about those people who made a difference. No matter where they are, here or in heaven, imagine how pleased those people are that you remember their gifts to you.

All of us have only one life to live. We can encourage, demean or cherish life in creative ways. Let us each resolve to be for others as the persons we remember were for us. Then we will assume our rightful place on the cycle of life.

Just when the caterpillar thought the world was over, it became a butterfly.

Please send your thoughts and stories to Dr. Lillian
Carson, 1187 Coast Village Road, Suite 1-316, Montecito,
CA 93108-1725
fax: (805) 565-1049 • email: *drlcarson@aol.com*
Web site *www.essentialgrandparent.com*

Resources

Legal Issues

Most laws regarding family law are state laws. Therefore, the laws governing divorce, custody, visitation and grandparent's rights vary from state to state. Information centers in other states may serve as resource guides and can be utilized for that purpose.

To determine the laws in your state contact the office of your State Attorney General listed below:

Offices of State Attorney Generals

Alabama	(334) 242-7300
Alaska	(907) 465-3600
	www.law.state.ak.us/
Arizona	(602) 542-5025
Arkansas	(501) 682-2007
California	(916) 445-9555
	JCM Legal Information—Torrance, CA (310) 212-5131
	Legal Information Line—Santa Barbara, CA (805) 965-8744
	Legal Information Mgmt—Redwood City, CA (650) 369-4944

Colorado	(303) 866-3617
	email: *attorney.general@state.co.us*
Connecticut	(860) 808-5318
	email: *attorney.general@po.state.ct.us*
Delaware	(302) 577-8400
Florida	(850) 414-3300
	Legal Information Ctr.—Gainesville, FL (352) 392-0417
	Legal Information Hotline Jacksonville, FL (904) 768-6016
Georgia	(404) 656-3300
Hawaii	(808) 586-1500
Idaho	(208) 334-2400
	www.state.id.us/ag
Illinois	(217) 782-1090
	www.ag.state.il.us
	Faxxon Legal Information SVC—Chicago, IL (312) 540-1170
	Faxxon Legal Information SVC—Springfield, IL (217) 522-3280
Indiana	(317) 232-4866
Iowa	(515) 281-5164
	www.state.ia.us/government/ag/
	email: *10waag@agmail.ag.state.ia.us*
Kansas	(785) 296-2215
Kentucky	(502) 696-5300
	www.law.state.ky.us
Louisiana	(225) 342-7013
	Legal Information Hotline—Baton Rouge, LA (225) 925-5297
Maine	(207) 626-8800

Maryland   (410) 576-6300
                  email: *oag@oag.state.md.us*

Massachusetts   (617) 727-2200

                  Men's Legal Referral Divorce—Norwood, MA
                  (781) 762-3329

                  United States Legal Referral—Marlborough, MA
                  (508) 480-0010

                  Legal Information Systems Inc.—Lexington, MA
                  (781) 860-5255

Michigan   (517) 373-1110

Minnesota   (651) 296-6196
                  email: *attorney.general@state.mm.us*

                  Legal Information SVC—St. Paul, MN
                  (651) 221-4441

Mississippi   (601) 359-3680
                  email: *msago l @ ago.state.ms.us*

Missouri   (573) 751-3321

                  Tel Law Legal Info SVC—St. Louis, MO
                  (314) 421-0255

Montana   (406) 444-2026
                  email: *mtattgen@counsel.com*

Nebraska   (402) 471-2682

Nevada   (702) 687-4170
                  www.state.nv.us/ag/
                  email: *aginfo@govmail.state.nv.us*

New Hampshire   (603) 271-3658

New Jersey   (609) 292-4925

New Mexico   (505) 827-6000

New York   (518) 474-7124
                  www.oag.state.ny.us

Legal Referral SVC Assn of Bar—New York, NY
(212) 626-7373

CCH Legal Info SVC—New York, NY
(212) 246-5070

Legal Information Tech—New York, NY
(212) 629-0941

N. Carolina (919) 716-6400

Excellent Legal Referral SVC—(910) 323-5266

N. Dakota (701) 328-2210

Ohio (614) 466-4320

Security Information Legal—Medina, OH
(330) 725-7252

Oklahoma (405) 521-3921

Christian Legal Referral SVC—(918) 225-7177

Oregon (503) 378-4400

Pennsylvania (717) 787-3391
www.attorney.general.gov

Legal Information Systems Inc.—Fort
Washington, PA (215) 542-9225

Rhode Island (401) 274-4400

Legal Information Referral SVC—Providence, RI
(401) 521-5040

S. Carolina (803) 734-3970
email: *contact@scattorneygeneral.org*

S. Dakota (605) 773-3215
email: *help@atg.state.sd.us*

Tennessee (615) 741-3491

Texas (512) 463-2100 *www.oag.state.tx.us*

Utah (801) 366-0260

Legal Information Bureau—Salt Lake City, UT
(801) 532-2443

Vermont	(802) 828-3171
	email: *aginfo@atg.state.vt.us*
Virginia	(804) 786-2071
	email: *oag.state.va.us*
Washington	(360) 753-6200
	email: *emailago@atg.wa.gov*
W. Virginia	(304) 558-2021
Wisconsin	(608) 266-1221
	email: *wisag@doj.state.wi.us*
Wyoming	(307) 777-7841

Mediation

An alternative to the legal system:

The Mediation Information and Resource Center
440 East Broadway, Suite 340
Eugene, OR 97401
(541) 302-6254
fax: (541) 345-4024

Visitation Issues

Grandparents Rights Center
723 W. Chapman Ave
Orange, CA 92868
(714) 744-8485
fax: (714) 744-4392

Custody

Help for parents without custody:

Grandparents Resource Center
P.O. Box 27064
Lakewood, CO 80227
phone and fax: (303)980-5707

Information for grandparents with custody:

Grandparent Information Center
American Association of Retired Persons (AARP)
601 E. Street, NW
Washington, DC 20049
(202) 434-2296
www.aarp.org

Resources For Substance Abuse

National Institute on Drug Abuse
www.nida.nih.gov/

Women and Drug Abuse
www.nida.nih.gov/WomensDrugs/Women-DrugAbuse.html

National Drug Strategy Network
www.ndsn.org/

Substance Use and Addiction Services
State by State Directory of treatment facts and general phone
numbers
www.ntc.org/public.htm

National Women's Health Information Center
800-994-WOMAN
Monday through Friday, 9 A.M. to 6 P.M., EST

Al-Anon
See local phone directory
www.al-anon.org/

Al-Anon Family Group Headquarters, Inc.
1600 Corporate Landing Parkway
Virginia Beach, VA 23454-5617
888-4AL-ANON
Monday through Friday, 8 A.M. to 6 P.M., EST

Alcoholics Anonymous
See local phone directory
www.alcoholics-anonymous.org/indes.html/

Other Grandparent Resources

Creative Grandparenting, Inc.
1003 Delaware Ave., Suite 16
Wilmington, DE 19806

Foundations for Grandparenting
400 Seventh St., NW, Suite 302
Washington, DC 20004-2206
(202) 783-0952

Grandparents Reaching Out (GRO)
Mildred Horn
141 Glen Summer Rd.
Holbrook, NY 11741
(516) 472-9728

National Coalition of Grandparents, Inc.
137 Larkin Street
Madison, WI 53705
(608) 238-8751

Newsletters

Hardcopy Publications

Dr. Lillian Carson's *Essential Grandparent Reading Circle
. . . for Grandparents & Others*
For free newsletter, send name, mailing address and the ages of
the children to whom you'll read to:

The Essential Grandparent Reading Circle
1187 Coast Village Road Suite 1-316
Montecito, CA 93108
fax: (805) 565-1049
email: *drlcarson@aol.com*

Some other newsletters are:

Grandparents Parenting . . . Again . . .
Phoenix Foundation
1500 W. El Camino, Suite 325
Sacramento, CA 95833
(916) 922-1615

Vital Connections
The Foundation for Grandparenting
7 Avenida Vista Grande
Suite B7-160
Santa Fe, NM 87505

Online Publications

Are You Raising Your Grandchildren? by Marianne Takas
http://www.fosterparents.com/index30raisinggrch.html

Grandparenting
http://ohioline.ag.ohio-state.edu/hyg-fact/5000/5213.html

Grandparents as Parents: A Primer for Schools
http://ericeece.org/pubs/digests/1996/dr-gra96.html

A Grandparents' Guide for Family Nurturing and Safety, by
T. Berry Brazelton and Ann Brown of the Consumer Product
Safety Commission
http://www.cpsc.gov/cpscpub/pubs/grand/grand.html

*It's Not the Same the Second Time Around: Grandparents
Raising Grandchildren*, by Renee S. Woodworth
http://www.zerotothree.org/2nd time.html

*Respite Services to Support Grandparents Raising
Grandchildren,* by Renee S. Woodworth
http://www.chtop.com/archfs45.html

*Things Grandparents, Neighbors, and Concerned Citizens
Can Do to Improve Education*
http://www.summit96.ibm.com/perspectives/citizenslist.html

Books for Parents and Grandparents

*The Good Divorce: Keeping the Family Together When Your
Marriage Comes Apart*
　　Constance Ahrons
　　Harper Perennial, 1994

In the Name of the Family
　　Judith Stacey
　　Beacon Press, 1996

Second Chances: Men, Women and Children a Decade After Divorce
Judith S. Wallerstein and Joan Berlin Kelly
Houghton-Mifflin Co., 1996

Child Custody Made Simple
Webster Watnik
Single Parent Press, 1997

Divided Families: What Happens to Children When Parents Part (Family and Public Policy, 1)
Harvard University Press, 1994

The Best Interests of the Child
Anna Freud, Albert Solnit and Joseph Goldstein
Simon & Schuster, 1998

Books for Children

Let's Talk About It: Divorce
Fred Rogers, Jim Judkis Illustrator
PaperStar, 1998
Reading level: Ages 4–8

Why Are We Getting a Divorce?
Peter Mayle, Arthur Robins and Peter Mayer
Crown Books, 1988
Reading level: Ages 4–8

Dinosaurs Divorce: A Guide for Changing Families
Marc Tolon Brown and Laurence Krasny Brown
Little Brown & Co., 1986
Reading level: Ages 4–8

Mom and Dad Don't Live Together Anymore
Nancy Lou Reynolds (Illustrator) and Kathy Stenson
Firefly Books, 1988
Reading level: Ages 4–8

Index

Help the Kids You Love, Love Books

*"If you read to a child 20 minutes a day, that child will hear **1 million** additional words a year and will gain **1,000** additional vocabulary words."*
—Delaine Easton, California State Superintendent of Schools

"Young children who are regularly and lovingly read to have a priceless advantage from the start. Every child deserves someone to share a book with, and what a wonderful 'someone' a grandparent is."
—Patricia S. Schroeder, President and CEO, Association of American Publishers

Join Dr. Lillian Carson's
Essential Grandparent™
Reading Circle
for Grandparents & Others
WHY + HOW + WHAT to read to kids

TM

The life you change may be your own!

Mail to: Dr. Lillian Carson, The Essential Grandparent Reading Circle
1187 Coast Village Road, Suite 1-316
Montecito, CA 93108-1725
fax (805) 565-1049   email *drlcarson@aol.com*

Yes, I want to change a child's life by becoming a reader. Enroll me in The Essential Grandparent Reading Circle and send my free newsletter. I understand there is absolutely no cost or obligation.

Name _____ Ages of kids _____

Mailing Address _____
Please Print Legibly   Street   City   State   Zip Code

Little Souls

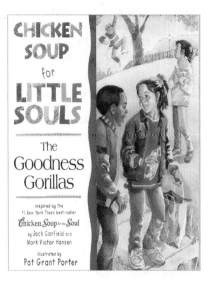

The Goodness Gorillas
The friends of the Goodness Gorilla Club have lots of great plans! But what will they do about Todd, the meanest kid in the class?
Code 505X, hardcover, $14.95

The Best Night Out with Dad
Danny has a new friend, and an important decision to make. Will he get to see the circus after all?
Code 5084, hardcover, $14.95

The Never-Forgotten Doll
Ellie wants to give a special gift to Miss Maggie, the best babysitter in the world. But everything is going wrong! How will she show Miss Maggie how much she loves her?
Code 5076, hardcover, $14.95

Available in bookstores everywhere or call 1-800-441-5569 for Visa or MasterCard orders. Prices do not include shipping and handling. Your response code is **BKS**.
Order online at www.hci-online.com

Inspire the Spirit

A Dog of My Own

Ben's wish comes true when his mom finally says he can have a puppy. But, on the way to pick up the puppy, Ben and his friend Kelly stumble upon a discovery that could change everything!
Code 5556, hardcover, $14.95

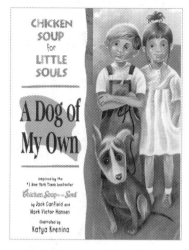

The Braids Girl

When Izzy helps Grandpa Mike with his volunteer work at the Family Togetherness Home, the girl in the corner with the two long braids makes a lasting impression on her. But, Izzy just can't seem to make the braids girl happy!
Code 5548, hardcover, $14.95

Della Splatnuk, Birthday Girl

The last thing Carrie wants to do is go to Della Splatnuk's birthday party. Everyone knows Della is weird, and Carrie's best friends have vowed not to go. But once Carrie is there, she begins to wonder whether Della is really all that bad, and whether all the kids who did not show up have ever given Della a chance.
Code 6005, Hardcover, $14.95

Remembering Mother, Finding Myself

"It all began with a whiff of perfume, a song and a search for a photograph. These commonplace things triggered memories deep within myself that started me on a journey to get to know the woman who was my mother for twenty-six years and who, on a spiritual level, is with me still."
—Patricia Commins

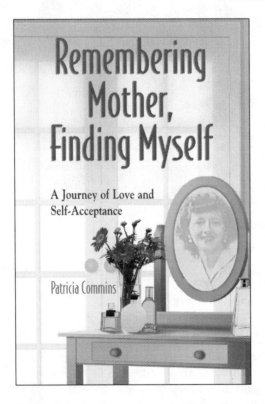

In this breakthrough book, author Patricia Commins, who lost her mother at 26, shows readers that the key to escaping the sorority of sorrow is by understanding their mothers as women and by feeling an ongoing connection with them.

Code #6668 Paperback • $11.95

Mourning and Dancing

Everyone grieves—some of us more than others, few of us well.

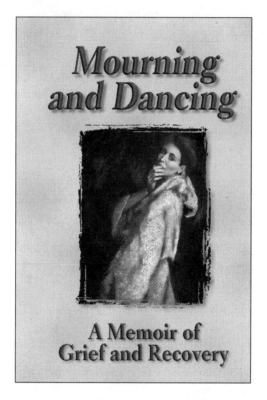

This moving story is the 30 year chronicle of a young widow and mother of two small children, who grieved poorly and finally discovered some truths about recovery and personal healing. It is much more than a personal statement - it will allow you to open your heart. When we allow ourselves to mourn, we celebrate the dance, and, in our hearts, life keeps beating.

Code #6714 Paperback • $10.95

Get Some Soup to Warm Your Heart

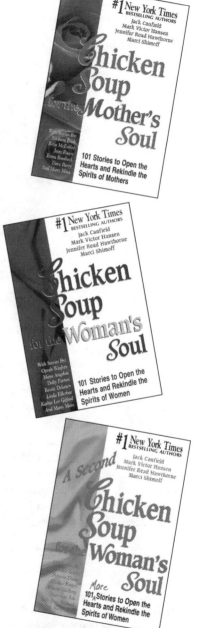

There are many ways to define a woman: daughter, mother, wife, professional, friend, student. . . . We are each special and unique, yet we share a common connection. What bonds all women are our mutual experiences of loving and learning: feeling the tenderness of love; forging lifelong friendships; pursuing a chosen career; giving birth to new life; juggling the responsibilities of job and family, and more.

These three volumes celebrate the myriad facets of a woman's life.

Chicken Soup for the Mother's Soul
Code #4606 Paperback • $12.95

Chicken Soup for the Woman's Soul
Code #4150 Paperback • $12.95

A Second Chicken Soup for the Woman's Soul
Code #6226 Paperback • $12.95

Also available in hardcover, audio cassette and audio CD.